Quandaries and Virtues

Quandaries and Virtues

Against Reductivism in Ethics

EDMUND L. PINCOFFS

UNIVERSITY PRESS OF KANSAS

Published by the University Press of Kansas (Lawrence, Kansas 66045), which was
organized by the Kansas Board of Regents and is operated and funded by Emporia
State University, Fort Hays State University, Kansas State University, Pittsburg
State University, the University of Kansas, and Wichita State University

Library of Congress Cataloging-in-Publication Data

Pincoffs, Edmund L.
    Quandaries and virtues.
    Bibliography: p.
    Includes index.
    1. Ethics. I. Title.
BJ1012.P56   1986   170   86-13352
ISBN 0-7006-0308-5

Printed in the United States of America
10   9   8   7   6   5   4   3   2

For Mary Elizabeth

Contents

Preface

Philosophers, peculiar creatures that they are, typically write alone in their studies. They are not given to joint research projects or the writing of books that have multiple authors. Yet, at the same time, they cannot do good work without the company of other philosophers, critically aware ones, against whom they can try out their ideas. I am no exception. I am greatly indebted to the persons on whom I have inflicted my ethical speculations in colloquies, lectures, and philosophical meetings. While I have mentioned in the notes persons who have been especially helpful in criticizing the individual papers from which these chapters emerged, I should also mention a few of the people whose criticism or inspiration extends beyond the particular chapters to the central notions of the book.

I have been wonderfully fortunate in my graduate students, too numerous to mention here, especially those who, in my spring 1984 seminar at the University of Texas on Virtue and Vice, read and discussed the first draft of this book. Many of the ideas in the book may have had their inception in weekly talks over many years with Konstantin Kolenda. My colleagues at the University of Texas have been uniformly helpful. I should mention in particular the late Hardy Jones, with whom I had long and exhaustive discussions, and Robert Solomon, who was kind enough to read the manuscript through and to offer useful and encouraging comments.

Robert Audi, Richard Rodewald, Alasdair MacIntyre, Thomas Seung, Douglas Browning, and Robert Simon have, at one stage or another, been particularly helpful critics or inspirations. Richard De George's competent and useful criticisms have been invaluable in the final revision. These names by no means exhaust the list of persons to whom I am indebted: I should also like to thank the many people not mentioned here with whom I have had good and useful discussions.

My thanks go not only to individuals but to institutions. I have, over the course of the last five years, received welcome research support from the University of Texas and fellowships from the National Endowment for the Humanities and the National Humanities Center. A part of the work on this book was done at Cambridge, and I owe further thanks to the President and Fellows of Clare Hall.

Few philosophical writers can long ply their trade without typists to convert rough drafts into smooth copy. Here I have been most fortunate. Coleen Kieke, the fine manuscript typists of the National Humanities Center, and Marian Webster have made remarkably error-free translations of sometimes cluttered pages into clean and neat ones.

I acknowledge, with thanks, the permission of the editor of *Mind* to republish "Quandary Ethics" as chapter 2; the editor of *The Monist* to republish parts of "Virtue, the Quality of Life, and Punishment" in chapter 5; D. Reidel Publishing Co. to republish part of "Two Cheers for Meno" in the same chapter; the editors of *The Individual and Society* to republish parts of "Personal Ideals and Moral Decisions" in chapter 7; and Routledge and Kegan Paul to republish "On Avoiding Moral Indoctrination" as chapter 8. Bibliographical details on these previously published essays are given in the footnotes to the mentioned chapters.

1

Introduction

> Were Socrates and Charles the Twelfth of Sweden both
> present in any company, and Socrates to say, "Follow me,
> and hear a lecture on philosophy"; and Charles, laying
> his hand on his sword, to say, "Follow me, and dethrone
> the Czar"; a man would be ashamed to follow Socrates.
> Sir, the impression is universal; yet it is strange.
> —James Boswell, *The Life of Samuel Johnson*

Ethics is a phoenix. It is a study that has lived a long life, has been obliterated (nearly) in the embers of neglect, and is now rising full-feathered from the ashes. It is time to ask whether the splendid new creature is a worthy successor of the old, less-gaudy bird.

The new bird is impressive. Workshops, institutes, myriad textbooks, monographs, journal articles, popular articles and books, new journals, new courses proliferate. Students crowd ethics lecture halls. Moral philosophers are on the staffs of hospitals, law schools, military institutions, and governmental agencies. Vast publishing projects collect the essays of the doctors, lawyers, economists, theologians, sociologists, philosophers, scientists, historians, and business-school professors who specialize in ethical studies. This is all in great contrast with the marginal existence of ethical studies during the first six decades of this century, when they were pursued largely in the back corridors of philosophy departments, published in a handful of articles and books, and read by a minuscule audience of philosophers, divines, and their students.

The complex reasons for the revival of moral concern in public and private life are not the business of this book. That concern is vivid and earnest, and I will assume that it is justified. In a time when rapid change is everywhere—in technology (especially medical), sexual mores, media-stimulated wants and expectations, social structure, natural environment, international relations—it is hardly surprising that there should be moral disorientation and a demand for whatever might be of use in achieving balance, reasoned consensus, common goals, common rules, and common understanding of what shape moral education should take.

Nor will I question the easily understandable turn toward ethics for help. Ethics is one of the longest-established disciplines in the intellectual repertoire of Western civilization. It was the prime philosophical subject for Socrates and was central for Plato and Aristotle, their pupils, and successors. It was a part of standard university education in the Middle Ages. It is a subject regularly taught (although until recently ill attended) in the philosophy departments, faculties, and schools of the Western world. What is more natural, then, than to assume that the place to go for help is to the experts, the people who know ethical theory and know how to apply it to the problems of the day?

But that is where I bog down, and where this book begins. Even though philosophers have long discussed the problem of free will, the 'good for man', practical wisdom, the nature of justice, courage, and benevolence, ethical theory is essentially a modern invention. To say that one has a theory of ethics is to say, as that term is usually understood, that one has a systematic account of the 'foundation' of moral judgment. Theories are made to be applied to cases, to provide the principles and procedures by which moral problems can be resolved. I will argue that the structures known as ethical theories are more threats to moral sanity and balance than instruments for their attainment. They have these malign characteristics principally because they are, by nature, reductive. They restrict and warp moral reflection by their insistence that moral considerations are related in some hierarchical order. I will argue that there is no such order.

I will hold that there are mutually irreducible types of moral consideration, that there is no hierarchy—with the king consideration at ease on the apex—no one-principle system that incorporates all of the moral rules. This will be unsettling to some of my readers. The metaphors (taken from the building trades) of a foundation or of an apex are powerful ones. Above all, in morals we want to be able to reason from something solid, unquestionable, beyond debate. It doesn't seem to matter whether the direction of reasoning is down from an apex or up from a foundation. The best way to loosen the grip of a metaphor is by means of a counter metaphor.

In thinking of the way that we reason about moral issues, think of nets. Nets are suspended by cords that run to points on the periphery. The strength of the net is the joint strength of the woven cords of which it is made and the points to which they lead. Think, then, of the leading types of moral consideration as points to which the cords run. One point will be the wrongness of injustice; another, the rightness of sympathy; a third, the wrongness of cruelty; and so on. To reason morally is to weave a net (or if fallacies crop up, to mend a net). To decide rationally is to compare the joint strength of one set of considerations to the joint strength of alternative sets. There is no formula for such comparisons. The ability to make effective comparisons must be cultivated. Some people will develop the kind of practical wisdom that will make their moral judgments especially worthy of respect. Others will not be good at moral reasoning, through defects of character or intellect. But the polemical point is that there are no moral experts.

There would be moral experts if the claims of ethical theory were true. There would be people who knew something that the rest of us do not know. They would know what the formula is by which we determine the difference between right and wrong, and they would know how best to apply it to cases that arise. Like experts in any field, we could divide our judgment of them into parts. We could acclaim their expertise while deploring their character. We could say that while they were really quite cruel, their judgment about moral matters was the best going. Or we could say that an unjust person is an authority on the justice of social practices. The point is that we could say these things without a halt, without the least concern that some special explanation is needed, some way of explaining away a seeming anomaly. But the seeming anomaly is a real one. Moral character and moral judgment are far more intimately bound together than theory advocates can allow. Moral judgment is an expression of the character of the person who offers it. This is not to say that because a person is of good character, we can trust his judgment in any circumstances that may arise.[1] He may not know enough about the facts of the case, may not be experienced in tracing out the causal lines to everyone affected by the course of action in question, or may just not be good at intricate thinking. It is not to say that experience of life and keenness of intellect are irrelevant when we think about whether Robin's moral judgment is to be trusted. But if that would be absurd, it would also be absurd to say that although Robin's character was rotten, her moral judgment was to be trusted—absent some special explanation.

The only special explanation that comes easily to mind is that moral judgment is being made synonymous with the capacity to think through to consequences for the general happiness, with the mechanical balancing of justice claims or with the tracing of the intricacies of quasi-legal rights claims. But while these capacities may be essential in some contexts, possession of them is far from guaranteeing sound moral judgment. To claim that it does would be to beg the question about rotten-character Robin. No matter how bright she may be or how good at intricacies, we can't trust her judgment. We can't trust it because she is not committed to finding just that balance of considerations that morality demands. To reduce moral reasoning to theory and application is, hence, tacitly to raise a question that should be, but is not, discussed by the advocates of theory: Are there moral experts?

The first part of this book, then, is a critique of overblown claims made on behalf of ethical theory. Three criticisms will be offered in as many chapters. The first is that there is no good reason to suppose that the subject of ethics need be confined to the resolution of difficult problems by the application of theory. The second and third question the relevance of theories to problems and the claimed justificatory powers of ethical theories. While these three chapters can hardly serve as a full-scale critique of a very large enterprise, they may at least stir doubt about the moral value of ethical theories.

If the cardinal sin of ethical theories is that they are reductive—that they eliminate by fiat what is morally relevant and legislate the form of moral reflection—then the question is whether a nonreductive discipline of ethics is possible. If moral reasoning and moral character are more intimately related than ethical theory allows, then there is the question of what account of morality can be offered that gives character its due. An answer to both of these questions is that the primary business of ethics ought to be with qualities of character, with the virtues and the vices. There are a great many such qualities, and recognition of them provides insurance against oversimplification of moral reasoning and moral life. In the second part of this book, I explore some of the implications of, and some of the booby-traps in, that answer.

The first of the chapters in this section takes up the question what it is that sets off the virtues and the vices from the long list of personality traits that includes them. I then criticize some arbitrary reductive definitions in contemporary writing on the ethics of virtue. In chapter 6, I argue that there can be a defensible form of perfectionism—a personal morality modeled on ideals of moral virtue. In chapter 7, I take up some of the difficulties in such a position, in particular the tensions between personal ideals and moral obligations.

In part 3, I consider, in two chapters, the question, crucial for any approach to ethics, of what its implications are for moral education. In the next-to-last chapter, I criticize some conceptions of moral indoctrination and of how and why to avoid it. In the final chapter, I sketch an approach to moral education for good character.

The overall argument of the last two parts is informed by a perspective on moral talk and reflection that I should try to make clear here. It is that such talk has uses and that if we are to understand it, we must ask what its uses are. (The plural is important, if we are ourselves to avoid reductionism.)

These uses of moral talk can, in turn, only be understood against a background of assumed facts about the common life of human beings. If human beings were radically different from what they are, then such talk, or varieties of it, might have no place, might not arise. If we had yolk sacs and carapaces as the result of genetic manipulations, then we might no longer be mutually dependent and vulnerable. Benevolence and sympathy might have no place. If we were no longer envious of one another's lot, if we no longer cared what share of the distribution of good things or bad ones we received, then we would have no occasion to cry injustice or to value justice. If we lived in a world in which our least desire was immediately fulfilled, then there would be no place for perseverance or fortitude. If we were immune to pain, psychological as well as physical, then there could be no cruelty. Benevolence, sympathy, justice, perseverance, and kindness are virtues only given certain facts about our common life. In the absence of those facts, these virtues have no place; they do not arise; talk of them or reflection on them has no use. They do not exist.

My perspective is, thus, a functional one, but I want to clarify in what sense it is functional. It is often assumed that functionalism and teleology necessarily go together. I am a functionalist, but I am not a teleologist. I think that if we are to understand moral talk and reflection, we must have some idea of their uses. But I do not want to issue pronouncements about the 'end of man'. That there can be non-teleological functionalism can best be seen by another excursion into metaphor. The functionalist perspective is that of the engineer, rather than that of the captain of the ship. Wherever the captain may want to go, the engine and working parts of the ship must operate well if he is to get there. We can say things about the optimum performance of the ship and about what is a necessary condition of optimum performance that presuppose nothing about the courses it is to follow. The steering gear must be in good order, as must the controls that lead to the engine, the engine itself, the lifeboats, and so on. We can also say some things about the common life aboard the ship: that it should not function in such a way that the participants in it are miserable, or anyway miserable beyond the necessities of getting the ship from here to there. To drop the metaphor, the virtues of persons and actions are qualities of their working well. But we do not need to know some supervenient common end before we can distinguish good from bad working, so long as we understand the *sorts* of ends that will be pursued and the conditions under which they are to be pursued.

To know what common human life is like is to understand such matters. To think of good functioning as functioning that is appropriate to the common life is to leave room for different ends that particular persons or groups may want to pursue within that situation. It is not to judge which of these ends is better or which should prevail. It *is* to rule out as permissible ends those that hinder the pursuit of other ends that are commonly pursued.

An alternative sea-going metaphor is that of a busy harbor. The harbor is functioning well if it is handling well the activities of ships according to the ends the ships are pursuing. A well-organized harbor will serve those ends well: loading and unloading and mooring and drydocking will go smoothly. The same sort of thing can be said about the virtues and vices of both persons and actions. They have to do with the good for man only in the sense that, given the goods that men tend to pursue, these qualities are desirable ones. They are desirable against the background of the common life, including the human tendencies that are aspects of that life.

What follows immediately is that as tendencies within common life or within the organization of common life change through history or across cultures, then what counts as a virtue or a vice will change. But there are limits. No one thinks that there will be a common human life in which justice, persistence, courage, and honesty will not be virtues—even though humility or aggressiveness, say, may be less appropriate in one era than in another.

There is another advantage in this common-life-functional perspective on moral thought and talk. It supplies an antidote to the kind of abstract individualism that characterizes too much of ethical thought. Individualism makes sense only against a background of social organization. There is no human situation that consists of an aggregate of unrelated individuals. We are social beings. We come into a world that is already organized; we are creatures of organization; we live in each other's lives; we understand ourselves through our reflection in the perceptions of others; we die in the lives of others. None of this is to say that we are socially determined, that we cannot meaningfully strive for our own perspectives on the common life, or that we cannot try to bring about social change—and sometimes even succeed.

Modern ethical theories typically suppose (explicitly in contract theory) that the most fundamental level of the human situation is an individualistic one: one in which there is either, as in Hobbes, a threat of war of all against all or in which, as in Rousseau, noble savages live free and independent lives, associating only for matters of individual convenience. In Kant, the individual wrestles alone with his conscience and legislates freely for himself, indeed universalizing for an aggregation of other imagined individuals, but only in the interest of noncontradiction in his own will. Mill's individual is an instrument for the common good, valuable only to the extent that he is effective in that single role—which is not a social role but a causal designation. This common individualistic tendency of the standard theories is indefensible. It rests on an unsupported and misleading premise: that the realm of ethics at bottom is a realm of nonsocially organized individuals, that social organization is not as much a fundamental aspect of the human situation as is gravity or the helplessness of a newborn child.

It is a misleading premise because it so effectively obscures the meaning of what has a far-stronger claim to be at the foundation of ethical thought: the fact that we must live together, we must live with each other in as effective, meaningful, fruitful, and harmonious a way as possible. Indeed, living together as well as possible means not living on top of or too tightly around each other. It means leaving a space for breath and time and creativity and thought. But this insistence on a collection of liberty rights makes sense only against a background of a society that is in place, in which the rights can be honored or dishonored. It is a social phenomenon: the demand for individual liberty, the insistence on the sanctity of the individual conscience, the guarantees of noninterference. It is a demand, an insistence, a guarantee, that makes sense only in a social context, not as the description of the way we really are.

If we must live together, then we must think not only about what we may do within the bounds of that common life but also about each other. We must, to find our way in our relations with each other, decide what we think about each other—whether to fear, to trust, to accept, to rejoice in, to love, to avoid, to approach, to enter into agreements with, to hire, to fire, to elect, to recall. This is the aspect of the human situation that is most central for ethics. It is the natural home of the moral concepts, including especially the dispositional terms that we call the virtues and the vices and, of those, especially the dispositions that bear on our conduct under common codes and standards.

Virtue talk arises where choices must be made of persons, of this person in preference to that one, or of whether to enter into this or that relationship or into a deeper relationship—under the social order, within social constraints. To have a virtue is to have a desirable disposition of a certain sort, a sort that I will speak about more specifically later. That a person has just that sort of disposition is a reason for preferring that person to other persons who do not have that disposition. If courage is a virtue, then that a person is courageous is a reason, all else being equal, to prefer that person to one who is not courageous.

Talk about responsibility, blame, guilt, excuses, and justifications has its natural home here too, because a necessary condition of making good choices between persons is that we know what behavior reveals their dispositions—what is and is not a false signal of a moral characteristic. The sudden gesture, the violent act, the apparently brutal accusation, may be excusable; it may be unrepresentative of the character of the agent. He may not, for a variety of reasons, have been himself; he may have misunderstood something; he may have done what he did accidentally; or whatever. On the other hand, the mere fleeting change of expression, the blurted utterance, or the unguarded gesture may be all too revealing.

I will try, then, to make clear, in different ways in this book, the extent to which ethical theories are seriously off target as accounts of moral life and of moral reflection and reasoning. By focusing on the abstracted-from-the-social-order individual and on the 'foundations' for decisions concerning what to do in a hopelessly abstract environment in which all that counts is consistency or supposed social contract or the happiness of everyone, ethical theories pass too easily over the topics that should be central in ethics. These are the radically different qualities of persons, policies, and actions and the ways in which the asserted presence or absence of these qualities count as considerations in weaving the nets of moral reasoning.

If this survey of topics is accused of being just another ethical theory, then at least it is not the reductivist sort of theory that is current in ethics and that is the target of this critique. It is more consistent with the interests of the long line of writers from Socrates forward who have concerned themselves with ethics. And it provides more usable guidelines for moral education. If these claims are even halfway true, then I have made a first step in what is a most important undertaking: providing an alternative in ethics to current conceptions of the subject. But the first task is to make clear the faultiness of those conceptions. To that task I now turn.

PART 1

Reductivism in Ethical Theory

Criticism is a study by which men grow important and formidable at very small expence. The power of invention has been conferred by nature upon few, and the labour of learning those sciences which may, by mere labour, be obtained, is too great to be willingly endured; but every man can exert such judgment as he has upon the works of others; and he whom nature has made weak, and idleness keeps ignorant, may yet support his vanity by the name of a critick.

—Samuel Johnson, *The Idler*, no. 60

2

Quandary Ethics

Ethics is everybody's concern. . . . Everyone . . . is faced with moral problems—problems about which, after more or less reflection, a decision must be reached.
—S. E. Toulmin, *Reason in Ethics*, p. 1

I ask the reader to start by supposing that someone (himself perhaps) is faced with a serious moral problem.
—R. M. Hare, *Freedom and Reason*, p. 1

What is ethical theory about? Someone might propose as an answer: "Everyone knows what an ethical problem is; ethical theory must be about the solutions to such problems." . . . But do we really know precisely what an 'ethical problem' is?
—R. M. Brandt, *Ethical Theory*, p. 1

My ultimate aim is to determine . . . how moral judgments can rationally be supported, how moral perplexities can be resolved, and how moral disputes can rationally be settled.
—M. G. Singer, *Generalization in Ethics*, p. 6

Only when he has linked these parts together in well-tempered harmony and has made himself one man instead of many, will he be ready to go about whatever he may have to do, whether it be making money and satisfying bodily wants, or business transactions, or the affairs of state. In all these fields when he speaks of just

I should like to thank Alasdair MacIntyre, Jon Moline, William Bennett, and Kurt Baier for criticisms. In an earlier form, this essay was published in *Mind*, n.s., vol. 80, no. 320 (Oct. 1971), and was reprinted in *Revisions: Changing Perspectives in Moral Philosophy*, ed. Stanley Hauerwas and Alasdair MacIntyre (University of Notre Dame Press, 1983).

and honorable conduct, he will mean the behavior that helps to produce and preserve this habit of mind. . . . Any action which tends to break down this habit will be unjust; and the notion governing it he will call ignorance and folly.

—Plato, *The Republic*

There is a consensus concerning the subject matter of ethics so general that it would be tedious to document it. It is that the business of ethics is with 'problems', that is, situations in which it is difficult to know what one should do; that the ultimate beneficiary of ethical analysis is the person who, in one of these situations, seeks rational ground for the decision he must make; that ethics is therefore primarily concerned to find such grounds, often conceived of as moral rules and the principles from which they can be derived; and that meta-ethics consists in· the analysis of the terms, claims, and arguments that come into play in moral disputation, deliberation, and justification in problematic contexts. It is my purpose in this chapter to raise some questions about this conception of ethics, which I shall refer to, for convenience and disparagement, as 'quandary ethics'.

Before proceeding to more philosophical matters it may be well to attend to rhetorical ones—to present considerations that might cause the reader to hesitate before replying, "Of course ethics is concerned to resolve problems on rational grounds! With what else would it be concerned? To abandon the search for rationally defensible rules and principles is to abandon moral philosophy," and so forth.

The first and most obvious rhetorical point is that quandary ethics is a newcomer, that the 'quandarist' is fighting a very long tradition with which he is at odds. Plato, Aristotle, the Epicureans, the Stoics, Augustine, Aquinas, Shaftesbury, Hume, and Hegel do not conceive of ethics as the quandarists do. If they are read for their theories—that is, for the grounds that they give for making particular difficult moral decisions—their teachings are inevitably distorted. To give such grounds, such justifications of particular difficult choices, was not their objective. They were, by and large, not so much concerned with problematic situations as with moral enlightenment, education, and the good for man. Again, the shift in emphasis is too patent to require documentation, but we may illustrate the point by means of a brief glance at the ethics of Aristotle.

He, as is well known, thought of ethics as a branch of politics, which in turn he thought of as a very wide-ranging subject having to do generally with the planning of human life so that it could be lived as well as possible. In the *Politics* the question concerns the best political arrangements, and a large and important preliminary is the comparative study of constitutions, so that one will know what kinds of arrangements are possible, with their advantages and disadvantages, so that a choice may be made. Similarly in ethics, the leading question concerns the best kind of individual life and the qualities of character exhibited by the man who leads it. Again, a necessary preliminary is the study of types of men, of characters, as possible exemplars of the sort of life to be pursued or avoided. This study occupies a large part of the *Nicomachean Ethics*. Moral problems are given their due but are by no means at stage center. The question is not so much how we should resolve perplexities as how we should live. Both the 'we' and the 'perplexity' or 'quandary' must be carefully qualified. The 'we' in question is not a mere place holder; rather, it refers to those of us who were well brought up, who have had some experience of life, who know something of the way in which the social order operates, who have some control over the direction of our lives in that we are capable of living according to a pattern and are not washed about by emotional tides or pulled hither and yon by capricious whim. So that if Aristotle is presented with a moral quandary, he has a right to presuppose a great deal concerning the upbringing, knowledge, and self-control of the persons concerned. But the notion of presenting Aristotle with a quandary is blurred if looked at through our spectacles. The kind of problems that Aristotle's qualified agents typically have are concerned not so much with what is to be done by anyone, qualified or not, in certain sorts of circumstances as with how not to fall into the traps that seize the unwary and convert them into one or another kind of undesirable character. When Aristotle discusses moral deliberation, it is not so much in the interest of finding grounds for the solution of puzzles as of determining when we may assign responsibility or of determining what it is that sets off practical from scientific reasoning.

But if Aristotle does not present us with quandaries into which the individual may fall and which he must puzzle and pry his way out of, this may be just because Aristotle does not value the qualities that allow or require a man to become bogged down in a marsh of indecision. There is, after all, the question of when we should and should not be involved in perplexities, when to avoid, as we often should, the *occasion* of perplexity. People can be perplexed because they are sensitive and conscientious, because they do not have the sense to avoid perplexity, or because they are pathologically immobilized by moral questions. A well-founded ethics would encourage the development of moral sensitivity but would discourage the entertainment of moral quandaries that arise out of moral ineptness or pathological fixation. The quandarists do not insist upon these distinctions, yet they are as important and obvious as the distinction between preventive and curative medicine. That the moral philosopher can be thought of as prescribing a regimen for a healthy moral life, rather than a cure for particular moral illnesses, would surely not be news to Aristotle.

The second rhetorical point to be made is that even though there may be philosophers who have thought through their reasons for accepting the present posture of ethics, very little argument can be found in defense of it. In fact, it rests, as far as I can tell, on unexamined assumptions that are perpetuated more by scholarly convention than by reasoned agreement. This posture, it may be well to emphasize, is not that of the casuist but one in which the ultimate objective of ethics is conceived to be the resolution of quandaries. It may be felt, indeed, that the nature of the times dictates what ethics must be and that therefore no critical examination of the role of ethics is in order. It may be believed that the era in which we live, beset by problems if men ever were, somehow militates in itself against any form of ethics but a problem-oriented one; that in this respect our time differs from all previous less-problem-plagued ones; that these problems are being loosed upon us by technological and social change; and that since change is so rapid and unpredictable, the best we can do for ourselves is to learn how to make decisions as they come along, to discover the form of a good decision; and the best we can do for our children is to teach them how to go about making decisions in the tight places into which they are sure to be crowded. This means that the tools for decision making must be put into their hands: the very general, and quite empty, principles from which rules that are appropriate to the occasion, whatever it is, may be derived. It may be felt, also, that the kaleidoscopic character of the times rules out an ethics focused, as such systems have been in most of the long tradition, on qualities of character and their development, since the inculcation of traits presupposes precisely the social stability that we do not have, because if we cannot count on social stability, we cannot know what character traits will be appropriate to the times in which our children will live.

This argument, which I have heard but not read, fails for two reasons, either of which is conclusive. The first is that it rests on a premise that is historically false. Character ethics has flourished in times of change that are comparable in their kaleidoscopic quality to our own. The Stoic ethic was taught and practiced over five hundred years, during which there were periods of violent change in the ancient world. These changes were often of such scope as to make individual citizens uncertain what kind of world their children were likely to inhabit. Athens, the original home of the movement, fluttered about in the surgings and wanings of empires, now moving forward with a democratic form of government, now languishing under tyrants supported by armies of occupation. The form that Stoicism took in Rome during the early empire, with its emphasis on the individual's control of his own soul no matter what the external circumstances might be like, is ample testimony to the insecurity that even the privileged classes felt in a time of tyranny and corruption.

The second reason is that the argument, even if it were sound, would militate as effectively against quandary ethics as against character ethics. Quandary ethics must, according to the argument, provide some stable means of arriving at decisions, no matter how circumstances may change. This is usually interpreted as requiring that rules and principles (or anyway 'good reasons') of universal application should be provided. But it is not at all clear why rules and principles will transcend change when qualities of character will not. If there are principles that would seem to apply in any conceivable world, why should there not exist qualities of character that are equally universal in scope? If there are character traits of narrower application, then there are principles that would be applicable in some circumstances but not in others. Indeed, it would be hard to imagine a world in which we should not make it a principle not to do to others what we would not want them to do to us; but it would be equally hard to imagine a world in which the quality of justice was without relevance. If there could be a world in which there was no place for justice, might there not also be a world in which there was no place for the Silver Rule? The argument works not so much to demonstrate the advantages of principles and rules in an uncertain world as to point up the limits of any form of moral education in times of change.

The rhetorical points, then, are that quandary ethics diverges from the main lines of discussion followed through most of the history of ethics and that there seems to be little offered in justification of this change of orientation—and that little is not convincing. Of course, it may well be that there are excellent reasons why ethics should now be focused on disputation, deliberation, and justification, to the exclusion of questions of moral character. At best, the rhetorical arguments can challenge the defender of the contemporary trend to produce those reasons.

But there are philosophical questions as well, questions that at least have the advantage that they point up some of the presuppositions of quandary ethics and at most reveal that indefensible distortions of ethics result from the contemporary fixation on problems and their resolution. Quandary ethics, remember, supposes that the ultimate relevance of ethics is to the resolution of the problematic situations into which we fall. The problems in question are practical, not philosophical. Moral philosophers, like other philosophers, must deal with philosophical quandaries, which are not escaped, although they may be emphasized or de-emphasized, by changing the focus of ethics. For example, questions about the logical status of 'moral assertions' will present as much of a problem for the nonquandarist as for the quandarist. But the assertions in question are as likely to be about ideal standards as about the duties and obligations that are incumbent upon everyone.

The questions I want to raise are: What is a problematic situation? and Who are 'we' who find ourselves in these situations? Discussion of these questions, however, will require that I rehearse briefly some time-honored distinctions.

The quandarist typically thinks of the problem question as What is the right thing to do? or What would be a good thing to do? or What ought I to do? But these questions are recognized to be ambiguous, at least in the sense that they fail to distinguish between queries concerning what is the morally *correct* (rule-required, expected, proper, appropriate, fitting) thing to do and queries concerning the morally *useful* (fruitful, helpful, practical, optimum) thing to do. The questions concerning rightness, goodness, and oughtness can be questions about correctness or usefulness, or both. The discussion of these questions is likely to be informed by general theories concerning correctness and usefulness: in particular the theory that the correct thing to do is the thing that it would be correct for any person in similar circumstances to do and the theory that the useful thing to do is the thing that will, directly or indirectly, increase the happiness and decrease the misery of everyone concerned as much as possible.

Now if we ask the quandarist what a moral problem is and who 'we' are who are enmeshed in the problem, certain difficulties arise for the quandarist conception of ethics. The quandarist might hold that a moral problem concerns what it is correct or what it is useful to do, or both. Whether he holds that correctness entails usefulness, or vice versa, need not concern us. Let us consider the correctness question, through the examination of a typical quandary.

I have made a promise, one of these promises encountered so frequently in the literature and so infrequently in life. It is to meet a friend to attend a concert. That is to say, I have solemnly averred, using the words, 'I promise', that this time I will not disappoint him, as I did the last time, and that I will indeed be on hand at eight o'clock at the theater. Meantime (back at the ranch) a neighbor calls to remind me of my agreement to attend an eight-o'clock meeting of the school board, to argue that a proposed desegregation plan is inadequate. What is the correct thing to do? How shall I decide? What is and is not relevant in my deliberations? Roughly: what is supposedly relevant is the agreements that I have made; what is supposedly not relevant is any personal wants or desires or characteristics that I may have. The question is whether a promise of this-and-that sort may be violated so that I may keep an agreement of that-and-that sort: whether anyone should violate the promise to keep the agreement, whether there is an exception to the rule that one should keep promises, or whether there is another, more stringent, rule that would justify my keeping the agreement and not the promise.

The analogy with the law is never far beneath the surface. A case in which I must decide whether or not to keep a promise is regarded as analogous to a case in which I must decide whether or not I have the right of way at an intersection. I have the right of way if I am approaching from the right. I must keep the promise if I have made it. There are, however, appropriate exceptions in both cases. I do not have the right of way, even though approaching from the right, if I have a 'yield' sign against me. I need not keep the promise, even though made, if to do so would result in my failing to keep an even-more-binding promise. For example, I need not keep a promise made in passing on a trivial matter, if to do so would result in my violating a promise made in great solemnity on a matter of real importance. In both the moral and the legal case, what count are the rule and its exceptions (or, understood differently, the rule and other rules with which it can conflict). What count as relevant are differences in the situation; what do not count as relevant are differences in the personal descriptions of the persons involved. In a court of law, that I am in a hurry to get home is irrelevant to the question of whether I have the right of way. That I am very fond of music is irrelevant to the question of whether I should keep the promise to attend the concert. What is relevant must have nothing to do with *me*, but only with the situation: a situation in which anyone could find himself. What is right for me must be right for anyone.

On the courtroom board, the model cars are moved through the diagramed intersection so as to represent the movement of the cars that collided. What are relevant are direction, signals given, signs, lighting conditions. Similarly we rehearse promise breaking. What are relevant are the nature of the emergency, the conflict of agreements, the likelihood of injury or damage if the promise is kept. These are relevant matters in that a general rule can be formulated governing any one of them. For example, it is a general rule that if a promise is a trivial one and if serious injury is likely to result from its being kept, then it need not be kept.

The analogy with law, with respect to the impersonality of the decision as to whether an action is or is not correct, is, I believe, widely accepted. It informs the quandarist conception of what a problematic situation is. According to this conception, it is irrelevant who the person is who is in the situation. Relevant, at most, are what tacit or explicit agreements he has made and what role—for example, father, employer, judge—he finds himself playing. The conflicts of rules or conflicts of duties are conflicts into which anyone can fall; and the resolution of the conflicts must be right for anyone who falls into them. This consensus seems to me to hide a confusion.

There is, in fact, an important disanalogy between moral and legal correctness decisions. There are considerations that are in a sense personal, that would be irrelevant in legal cases, but that are relevant in moral ones. They have to do with what the agent will allow himself to do and to suffer in accordance with the conception that he has of his own moral character. The quandarist cannot, I think, ignore these considerations; but to give them their due is to shift the focus of ethics away from problematics toward character—away from Hobbes and toward Aristotle.

The moral question, inevitably, is What would it be correct for me to do? It may be, indeed, that I cannot both keep my promise to my friend and my agreement with my neighbor. So, I will have to decide. Say I decide to keep the agreement. How can I justify this decision to my friend? If I can do so at all, I must make use of principles that I set for myself, but not necessarily for other people, and of moral ideals that I have but that I do not necessarily attribute to other people. I must justify myself to him for what I have done. I cannot do this by talking only about what anyone should have done in the same circumstances. Indeed, if what I did would have been wrong for anyone in the same circumstances to do, then it would have been wrong for me. If there had been no conflicting agreement and if I simply broke the promise to avoid the perturbation of my soul that would likely have been caused by rushing to be on time, then I decided incorrectly. But *it does not follow that because my decision would have been right for anyone in the same circumstances, it would have been right for me.* It follows only that almost no one could rightly blame me for what I did, that what I did was permissible. But I can blame myself. Those persons who are close enough to me to understand and to share my special moral ideals can blame me too.

Suppose that I have devoted my life to the cause of desegregation, that all of my spare time and energy and means are devoted to it. Suppose that I have taken a particular interest in the development of school policy in my town. Suppose that it is a part both of my self-conception and of the conception that others have of me that I could not miss an opportunity to press the cause of desegregation, that if I did so I would have to question my own integrity as a person. Suppose that I know that this particular meeting of the school board is a crucial one, one at which the final decision on a plan will be made. Suppose that I am recognized as the chief spokesman for the cause of meaningful desegregation. Suppose that I have built a deserved reputation with others and with myself for persistence and courage in the face of obstacles, for being a man of principle, for sensitivity to the needs of others. Then what would be right for someone else in a situation in which a solemnly given promise conflicts with an agreement to attend a meeting might well not be right for me. If my personal ideals and my conception of myself as a moral person are to be excluded from consideration as merely personal and if nothing is to remain but considerations that have to do with the situation as it would appear to anyone regardless of his former character, then the decision process has been distorted in the interest of a mistaken conception of ethics. The legal analogy has been taken too seriously.

It is easy to be misunderstood here. I am not glorifying the prig, nor do I intend to offer him comfort. I am not suggesting that the person who takes into account his ideals of character should agonize in public over them or that he should be pointedly or even obnoxiously rigid in his adherence to his standards. In fact, his ideals of character may rule out priggishness too. Nevertheless, even though he should not take his ideals inappropriately into account, he should take them into account.

But suppose the quandarist is quite willing to allow all of the sorts of considerations that I have mentioned in the previous paragraph. Suppose he insists that there is nothing inherent in his conception of ethics as being focused upon the resolution of moral difficulties that prevents him from taking these matters into account. Well, fine! That is all that I am arguing for. Then ethics must take seriously the formation of character and the role of personal ideals. And these matters must be discussed at length before decision making is discussed. Moral decision making will no longer appear in the literature as an exercise in a special form of reasoning by agents of undefined character.

But the quandarist might take a different tack, arguing that the distinction between considerations having to do with the situation and considerations having to do with the character of the agent breaks down. "Why should not my formed character be a part of the situation?" he might ask. My response must be a qualified one. In courts of law, such a distinction is maintained, even though it may not always be clear what is and is not relevant to the issue of guilt (that is one reason we must have judges). In the 'court of morals' we maintain it fairly well, although there is a wide twilight zone between the two. But again, this is an objection that works more in my direction than in his. To whatever extent it is impossible to maintain the distinction, to that extent we must pay more attention in ethics to character and its formation.

The general point I have made is that what would be right for anyone in the same circumstances (understanding 'circumstances' to refer to what in law would be the 'collision situation' only, but not to refer to what is 'merely personal') is not necessarily right for me. Because I have to take into account, as well as the situation, the question of what is worthy of me. What may I permit myself to do or suffer in the light of the conception I have of my own so-far-formed and still forming moral character?

It may be useful in expanding this point to return for a time to the concept of rules. It is here that the legal analogy has the strongest grip on the imagination. We say to ourselves: If I want to know what is the correct thing to do, then I must know whether there is a rule that covers this situation—or two rules or a rule and an exception. But even if—which I would deny—we are tied by some kind of logical necessity to the concept of rule abiding in thinking what is and is not correct, we would still have to let in considerations of character by the back door. Let me explain.

To do so, it is necessary to distinguish between different ways in which a rule may come to bear upon an agent. An analogous distinction could be made for prescriptions. In the armed services, as I remember dimly from an ancient war, it is customary to distinguish between orders and commands. A command tells us what to do or to refrain from doing in such explicit terms that there is either no or very little room for variation in the way in which it is obeyed or disobeyed. An order, on the other hand, does not so much specifically tell us what to do as what to accomplish or at what we should aim. "Report at 10.00" is a command; "Provide protective screen for the convoy" is an order. There can, of course, be general and standing orders and commands. A general command would be "All hands report at 10.00 tomorrow morning," and a general standing command would require all hands to report every morning at 10.00. "Exercise extreme caution when in enemy waters" can serve as a general standing order. General commands and orders apply to everyone; standing orders and commands apply to recurrent situations. Rules may be like general standing commands or like general standing orders; analogously, they may be like general standing specific and nonspecific prescriptions. They may allow no leeway in compliance, or they may allow a great deal of leeway.[1]

Some moral rules are more like general standing orders than like general standing commands: for example, "Love thy neighbor" or "Do not cause suffering." They say what is wanted but do not say what to do. If, however, we concentrate upon rules that are like commands, such as "Do not kill" or "Never break promises," we are likely to think of moral rules much like criminal laws, in that they will consist, for us, largely of specific injunctions and directions. But if we recognize that they can also be like orders, we will be more aware of the discretion they sometimes allow. They do not tell us exactly what to do so much as they indicate what we should struggle toward in our own way. But since we are already moral beings with characters formed, the way in which I will abide by an order/rule is not the same as the way in which you will. In fact, I have to decide not only what the rule is that governs the case but also how to go about honoring it. In deciding this, it is inevitable that I will not approach the problem in a vacuum, as any anonymous agent would, but in the light of my conception of what is and is not worthy of me. So, considerations of character, of my own character, do enter in by the back door, even if, as I have assumed for the sake of argument, the notion is that being moral is nothing but following a set of moral rules.

Personal considerations, then, in moral decisions, as opposed to legal decisions, need not be merely personal. It is often not irrelevant to the correctness of my moral decision that I take into account what I am—the conception that I have of myself as a moral being. In fact, the recognition of these considerations of worthiness leads us away from the typical examples of quandary ethics. We may now also consider not so much examples in which the individual is faced with a quandary concerning what he should do as ones in which he is reacting as an admirable moral character would to a situation that might call forth less admirable responses on the part of another. He turns the other cheek, walks the second mile, storms the impossible bastion, exhibits his finely tuned sense of justice by his decision, refrains from pleasurable recreation until the last job of his work is done. He exhibits his character in doing these things: he shows forth the kind of man that he is.

Now it might be said, in weary professional tones, that I have simply insisted upon a distinction that is quite familiar to the contemporary moral philosopher—the distinction, which has been with us at least since Aristotle, between the rightness of the act and the praiseworthiness of the agent. The act, it will be said, may be right, even though the agent is not necessarily praiseworthy for having done it. Or it will be said that I have failed to distinguish between obligation and supererogation: that what a person is obliged to do is one thing, but that if he is a saint or a hero, he may of course exceed the demands of duty and be accorded a halo or a garland, as the case may be.

In response, I want to say that both of these distinctions, while in other ways useful, may lead us to miss the point that I want to make. Consider first the distinction between the rightness of the act and the praiseworthiness of the agent. I want to insist that the question of whether the act is right may only with care be severed from the question of whether the agent is praiseworthy. The agent earns praise by doing what, in his lights, is only right, by doing what he could not conceive of himself as not doing. In considering whether the action is right, he brings in considerations beyond those of the generalizability of a rule. He wants to know not merely whether anyone may do it but also whether he may. Indeed, we would not blame him for failing to go the second mile, but from his standpoint he is convinced that this is what was right for him to do. He, in fact, exhibits himself as the moral character that he is by the demands that he makes upon himself and by his taking it for granted that these demands must be met.

Now take the distinction between obligation and supererogation. Again, it does not follow that because a person has more guide rails than the rules that in his opinion should apply to everyone, he is either a saint or a hero, that he is morally extraordinary. In fact, a person's character is likely to exhibit itself in his making obligatory for himself what he would not hold others obligated to do. A person does not attain moral stature by what he demands of others but by what he demands of himself; that he demands more of himself than others is not something in itself admirable, but is what is to be expected if he is to have a distinct moral character. The question of whether an act would be right for anyone in the same circumstances can show only that it would be permissible for everyone or that it would be mandatory for everyone. What is permissible or mandatory for everyone is so for the moral man, but even leaving aside the question of leeway discussed above, he may not consider it right for him to do what would be permissible for anyone, or he may regard it as mandatory for him to go the second mile, rather than merely the first, which is mandatory for everyone. The question of what is right for anyone in the same circumstances therefore provides the agent with but the beginnings of an answer to the question of what he should do.

The special requirements that I place upon myself in virtue of the conception that I have of what is and is not worthy of me must not be confused, either, with the special requirements incumbent upon me in virtue of "my station and its duties." There, requirements deal with duties that I have as a father, a judge, a village lamplighter, a sergeant at arms, or what have you. Again, these are in the realm of the minimal requirements that should be met by anyone: anyone, this time, who falls into the same role as I do.

Quandary ethics, then, conceives of a quandary that arises because I fall into a certain situation. The situation is such that it can be described in perfectly general terms, without any reference to me as an individual, including my personal conceptions of what are and are not worthy deeds and attitudes and feelings—that is, worthy of me. I may, according to this conception, fall into the situation in virtue of my falling under a rule that would apply to any person or in virtue of my falling under a rule that would apply to any person playing a particular role. The general situation is what gives rise to the quandary; and it is only by reference to the features of the situation that I may deliberate concerning what I should do or that I may justify my action. Just as I may refer only to the position of my car at the intersection and not to my personal standards or ideals, so I may refer only to the promising and to the nature of the emergency that caused its violation, with no reference to my standards or ideals. But I contend that reference to my standards and ideals is an essential, not an accidental, feature of my moral deliberation. An act is or is not right from my standpoint, which is where I stand when I deliberate, not merely as it meets or fails to meet the requirements of an ideal universal legislation, but also as it meets or fails to meet the standards that I have set for myself. I am not judged morally by the extent to which I abide by the rules (those which are like general standing commands) which set the minimal limits that anyone should observe in his conduct, even though it may be a necessary condition of my having any degree of moral worth that I should abide by such rules.

The person who is concerned in nonstupid and non-pathological ways over what he should and should not do is, to that extent, a conscientious person. Quandary ethics is addressed to the conscientious person. He is its ultimate customer. But two things should be said here: that the truly conscientious man is concerned not just with what anyone should do but also with what he should do (this I have discussed) and that conscientiousness is but one feature of moral character. Loyalty, generosity, courage, and a great many other qualities may figure as well. We cannot identify morality with conscientiousness. This, I charge, is what quandary ethics does. By starting from problems and their resolution and by confining the description of problematic situations to those features of which a general description can be given, the whole of the question of morality of character is restricted to judgments concerning the conscientiousness of the agent. Since it may be somehow possible to reduce being moral to being conscientious, we should examine the plausibility of such a reductivist claim. But it is worth mentioning that the quandarists do not so much as recognize as such the question of what gives conscientiousness the sole claim to moral worth. It is worth repeating that in speaking of conscientiousness, we are not speaking of those degenerate forms, seldom recognized by the quandarist, in which there is a mere moral dithering (the Buridan's Ass Complex) or in which there is a seeking out of occasions for moral puzzlement when there is no real ground for such puzzlement (pathological conscientiousness).

Why is it, then, that conscientiousness gets the nod from contemporary moral philosophers over such qualities as loyalty, integrity, and kindness? Why would not honesty have equal claim to consideration? Or sensitivity to suffering? The answer may be obvious to others, but it is not so to me. I suspect that the best answer would take the form of an historical-sociological disquisition upon the increasing complexity of the social order, the increase in the possibilities of breakdown and disorder, the resultant need for more and more complex rules, and finally, the consequent demand for the kind of individual who will not only be rule abiding but also 'rule responsible', in that he does not flap, panic, or throw up his hands when—as is inevitable—the rules conflict in a given situation in which he may find himself. He should be rule responsible also in that where there is no rule to govern a given choice, he will create a rule that is consistent with the other rules that he accepts, and in that he has at heart the attainment of a community governed by an ideal set of rules, and that he evinces this interest in the legislation for himself of rules that would be consistent with the rules governing such a community. Such a person would have an intense regard for rules—for the enactment, interpretation, and application of them. This regard would extend not only to 'public' rules—rules that govern everyone's action in recurrent situations—but to 'private' rules as well—rules that result from particular relationships with other persons into which he voluntarily enters. These rules, which might be distinguished from others by being called 'obligations', rest on tacit or explicit commitment to do or refrain and require constant interpretation, since the implications of our commitments in future contingencies are often far from clear at the time when we make them (e.g., "Love, honor, and obey," ". . . help you get started").

Surely the disquisition need not extend farther. It could easily be expanded into a convincing case for the importance of rule responsibility in our culture. But it would show at best that one desirable, even socially necessary, quality is rule responsibility, or conscientiousness. It does not have the consequence that we must confine our assessments of moral character to judgments of the extent to which the individual is rule responsible.

Suppose that a person wants to know what he should do about the moral education of his children. What will he learn from the quandarists? He will learn, as might be expected, that he should teach them how to make decisions: that is, according to one popular version, he will impart to his children as stable a set of principles as is possible in the changing circumstances in which he lives; but he will also give them the idea that they must learn to make their own decisions of principle when the occasion arises, even though he cannot teach them how to do so. We later learn that the principles in question must be universalizable prescriptions, applicable to any persons similarly situated. But is moral education best understood as teaching children how to make moral decisions? One might also reply that the problem of moral education is not so much teaching children how to make moral decisions as giving them the background out of which arise the demands that decisions be made. The focus of moral education might well be, not so much decisions, as the inculcation of excellences of character. The adult of good moral character must indeed be able to handle difficult situations as they arise and to reason about problems unforeseeable by his parents; but to reason well, he must already be an adult of good moral character: loyal, just, honest, sensitive to suffering, and the rest. Everything is not up for grabs! Unless he has these qualities, moral dilemmas will not arise for him. Unless he has a well-formed character, his prescriptions for himself and others are not likely to be morally acceptable. It is, as Aristotle notes, the prescriptions of qualified moral agents to which we should bend our ears.

One aim of moral education that the quandarists are apt to overlook is the development of the sense of the moral self as the product of continuous cultivation. It is as a formed and still-forming self that one either confronts or properly avoids moral problems. There are no moral problems for the child whose character is yet to be formed. For the quandarist, problems may arise for anyone at whatever stage of development he may be, when there is a conflict of rules or principles. What is socially essential is that there should be a workable and working set of rules and that there should be principles that can serve as arbitrators between them. The argument that there is a need for such rules and principles is inevitably a Hobbesian one. But precisely the source of the discomfort with Hobbes was that he approached ethics from this administrative point of view. He abandoned the cultivated moral self and insisted on reducing ethics to a code of minimal standards of behavior, standards that cannot be ignored without social disaster.

Very close to the surface in quandary ethics is the presupposition that there is an essence of morality—that being moral can be reduced to being rule responsible. But no more reason exists to believe that there is an essence of morality than that there is an essence of beauty. The suspect notion that there is an essence of morality is confused with the defensible idea that some moral rules are socially essential. However men may conceive their moral characters, whatever moral education they may have had, whatever moral models they may hold dear, whatever may be their religious beliefs, whatever virtues they may consider paramount, it is socially essential that they should be rule responsible. But to grant that rule responsibility is socially essential is not to grant that it is the essence of morality, in that all other moral character traits can be reduced to or derived from some form of this one. We may, even if we hold to the administrative point of view, expand our list of socially necessary character traits beyond rule responsibility. Chaos also threatens in the absence of tolerance, temperance, and justice, for example. These, too, are socially essential virtues.

To say that they are socially essential is to speak elliptically. What is essential is that everyone should exhibit some virtues to a certain degree and that some persons should exhibit others to a certain degree. It is not essential that everyone be as honest as Lincoln, nor is it essential that anyone but judges or others who have something to distribute should be just in any degree, since the opportunity for justice or injustice does not otherwise arise. It is clearly socially essential that everyone should be rule responsible to a degree commensurate with the complexity of the society; and it is socially desirable that everyone should be rule responsible to as high a degree as possible and that moral models or prophets should show the way. But it does not follow from any of this that morality can be reduced to rule responsibility. The attempt to reduce moral character to any given trait by philosophical fiat is open to suspicion. Individuals may, and perhaps should, give focus to their moral lives by centering them around some particular virtues—for example, honesty or sensitivity to suffering. But to contend that morality is nothing but honesty or sensitivity to suffering is to attempt to legislate for everyone what cannot be legislated. We may encourage children and ourselves in the development of certain virtues, but the form that each person's character assumes will inevitably be the result of his own selective cultivation and his own conception of what is and is not worthy of himself. It is, once we move beyond the minimal needs of society, his problem, peculiar to him, his training, and his ideals. To insist otherwise is to espouse the cause of the moral leveler.

The remark that certain virtues are socially essential is also elliptical in that it fails to distinguish between virtues that are essential, to a certain degree, in all or some men and to the very existence of any social order and those that are essential to the continued existence of a particular social order. The distinction is, as Hobbes recognized, a crucial one. 'Gentility', as that term was understood in the pre–Civil War South, was necessary to the existence of the social order created by white landholders. When the nongentile Snopses appeared, that social order collapsed. It may be that people are either so attached to a particular social order or so averse to another that they are willing to entertain the possibility of the absence of any social order, rather than see the one collapse or the other prevail. This is social nihilism, but it does not entail moral nihilism. The individual may prize non-socially-essential virtues over socially essential ones. In the interest of the continued existence of society, we cannot allow such moralities to prevail.

Earlier I distinguished between questions of correctness and questions of usefulness. I have confined my discussion to the former sort of question, but it could be extended with little difficulty to the latter. Suppose that the conception of decision making is that it has to do with the best way to use the circumstances, to take advantage of the situation, to maximize the happiness of everyone concerned. Again, the question will be, not What should I—in the light of my moral character and ideals—do? but What might anyone who finds himself in this situation most usefully do? It is a question about means to ends: a question not about how I might be most useful in the circumstances but about how anyone might increase happiness. Conceived this way and supposing the goal of happiness to be one that we all understand in the same way, then the question of what I should do is not a moral question at all; it is one that could best be answered by a social engineer familiar with the circumstances. Even if the question of what would be the most useful does not trail behind it a general theory to the effect that there is only one kind of thing that is ultimately useful, and if the possibility that there are a great many useful kinds of things that one may do is left open, as it should be, there is still a tendency to regard the question of what 'one' may do which is most useful in a given 'situation', as if it could be answered without regard to the moral character of the agent. Again: granting that the promotion of a given state of affairs would be useful and that a given line of action would promote that state of affairs, it might seem to follow that I should undertake that line of action. It does not. All that follows is that it would be generally desirable if I, or anyone, should. But in the light of the commitments, interests, and tendencies that I have already developed, it might seem a great deal more desirable that I should follow some alternative course of action. It might be generally desirable that I—and others— should join in a general demonstration against a war; but it might be more desirable that I should follow my already developed moral commitment to the abolition of capital punishment. I cannot decide what would be most useful without taking into account my conception of myself as a committed moral agent who has already for some time been active in the world.

Hegel suggests that an approach to understanding a philosophical view may be to find out what, on that view, are the chief obstacles to overcome. The chief obstacle for the quandarist who is faced with a moral perplexity is, I think, the void. It is the nightmare realm in which we can find no ground as heavier and disconcertingly heavier burdens descend upon us. The chief problem is how to find footing. The existentialists create the footing—harden thin air. The naturalists and intuitionists claim to discover it where intelligent men had somehow missed it before. The subjectivists fashion it out of their own approval. None of this is very plausible. We must ask, not how we find ground in the void, but why we think that we are in one. Who are 'we' who are supposed to be in a void? Are we not concerned to find answers to our repeated demands for ground? We are not then morally featureless, but we have concerns. The intuitions are ours; the discoveries are ours; the introspection is ours. We are not disembodied, historyless, featureless creatures. We are beings who have developed to a point and have even cultivated ourselves. The problems that we face must qualify as problems for us, must be our problems. It makes a difference who we are. We cannot describe the problem by describing an anonymous collision situation. Aristotle did not give open lectures; St. Paul did not write open letters. When they used the word 'we', they spoke from within a community of expectations and ideals: a community within which character was cultivated.

In part, the problem of the featureless 'we' arises out of the sense that somehow a universal ethic must be created. The 'must' is a Hobbesian one: it is socially essential. But if we create a universal ethic it must, it seems, be for abstract, general man—the man who has no special features, moral or otherwise. But it does not follow that an ethic that is for the man who has no special features is for the man who has none. It is precisely these special features that are likely to give form to the perplexities that arise. They arise for us, but not in a void.

It might seem as if they could arise in a void in which considerations of our own character-defined possibilities and impossibilities are irrelevant, if we fix our gaze on quasi-legal, collision-situation paradigms—on what seem to be moral general standing commands, such as "Keep promises" or "Don't kill." But even if these bare rules be admitted as moral, one could hardly give an acceptable account of moral quandaries by reference to them alone. For in the first place, there are also general standing moral orders, which give us vast scope in application; and secondly, there are the perplexities that arise quite outside of the supposedly rule-governed realm of morals—perplexities that come about because of the conflict of commitments and ideals that I as a moral agent have.

To take the resolution of problems as central while conceiving of problems on the collision model is indefensibly reductivist. It reduces the topic of moral character to the topic of conscientiousness, or rule responsibility. But it gives no account of the role of the character as a whole in moral deliberation; and it excludes questions of character that are not directly concerned with the resolution of problems.

It may be useful, in closing, to mention some things that I am not claiming. My position is not the subjectivist one that whatever seems right to me is right. Universalizability does provide a test for the rightness of my action, but it sets only minimal requirements, and these often in such fashion as to leave me a range of ways in which I can meet them. I am not claiming that an interest in finding grounds for the resolution of moral problems is the wrong door through which to enter ethics. But there can be more than one door; and the house is a larger one than the quandarists would lead us to believe. I am not insisting that every moral agent must be a saint or a hero or some combination of both but only that his moral character cannot be defined solely by reference to his conscientiousness in finding the appropriate rules of the road or the appropriate means to a common end. I do not contend that all that should count in moral deliberation is whether the proposed action would be acceptable to me in the light of the moral conception that I have of myself. I must first ask what would, in this or any similar situation, be mandatory or permissible for anyone. But this is not all that I must ask. To hold, or to presuppose, that it is, is to adopt an indefensibly narrow conception of the subject of ethics.

How have we come to narrow the subject so? Why have we become reductivists in a field historically so rich and complex as that of ethics? Perhaps it is because, in our fixation on quandaries, we have invented the notion that there are instruments by means of which quandaries can be analyzed, dissected, and resolved: ethical theories. Perhaps it is because, with such instruments in hand, we make uses of them and claims for them that far exceed their capacity.

I turn, then, in the next two chapters, to two questions about ethical theories: How can they be relevant to moral problems? and How, supposing relevance, can a theory justify a moral conclusion?

3

The Relevance of the Standard Theories

Ethical theories are supposed to give us handles on moral problems—to help us recognize and understand them and give us the means to resolve them. If we are to assess an ethical theory as more or less successful in dealing with moral problems, then we ought to be able to state the moral problems independently of the theory. The theory should not itself be appealed to in determining what a moral problem is. That is what I suspect happens in what I will call the standard ethical theories: utilitarianism, Kantian formalism, and contract theories.[1]

It might seem as if it is unfair to demand that the problem be specifiable independently of the ethical theory. It might be argued by analogy that if we are to resolve a scientific problem, then we must learn to state problems in the appropriate scientific terminology—of chemistry or physics or whatever—before we can do anything about them. If fish are dying in the bay, then we must talk in the appropriate ways about pollution sources, chemical compositions, and water levels and movements. It is only in these terms that we can approach a solution, such as the reduction of introduced chemicals, neutralization, or channeling. The problem, it might be said, *is* a scientific one, only it is first stated in an unscientific way. Chemistry tells us, so it might be argued, not only how to approach the problem but also what kind of problem it is.

I should like to thank Robert Solomon, Robert Simon, and Barbara Levenbook for their detailed comments on this chapter.

We do not, however, need to know all about channeling, chemical composition, and neutralization to know that shoals of silver fishes are reeking on the shore. It is the litter and the reek that leads us to find help in chemistry, biology, and oceanography. We know what we want when we go to the chemists. Because they understand what the problem is, they can translate it into scientific terms. It is a scientific problem in the sense that it is better approached scientifically than through ritual and shamans, not in the sense that there is no problem until the chemical and physical theories are brought to bear. To bear on what? The problem, of course. If one theory about why perch are sensitive to phosphates proves to be incorrect, we look for another that will forward our inquiry. The problem remains constant.

Contrast this scientific paradigm with an ethical one. From the way in which moral philosophers often speak, one would suppose that there are moral problems, and that there are alternative theories about the best way to approach them. (See the table of contents in nearly any "applied ethics" collection of readings.) But it soon turns out that what is to count as a moral problem is determined by the theory. How is a moral problem to be stated? As an inconsistency in the rules that one 'legislates'? As a difficulty in the maximization of happiness? As a question about the force of supposed social contracts? The standard ethical theories are erected on such considerations. If there is no problem about the maximization of happiness or about the minimization of misery, then, for the utilitarian, there *is* no moral problem, however much people may speak of moral intuitions, conflicts of duties, or whatnot. If for the Kantian there is no question of what the rules of duty require, there is no moral problem, no matter the talk about consequences. For the contractarian, moral problems arise only in the application of the terms of the contract to the given circumstances. An essentialism is at work here that is worthy of investigation.

Writers on moral philosophy certainly suppose that it is possible for the advocate of one of the standard ethical theories to recognize as a moral problem what would be a problem for advocates of another, an inconsistent, theory. They tell us, for example, that the 'problem of punishment' is a crux for utilitarianism and retributivism, incompatible theories, neither one of which seems to provide satisfactory resolutions.[2] But is the utilitarian problem the *same* problem as the retributive one? The problem for the utilitarian is to answer the charge that it is morally wrong to cause anyone unhappiness, since only the general happiness can justify that. The retributive problem is that we are entitled to inflict punishment only when it is deserved and that we must therefore show that what was inflicted was deserved. But why, then, should we say that the utilitarian problem of punishment and the retributive one are the same? In both cases, their referring to the intentional infliction of suffering or misery is contingent. The utilitarian reason for worrying about making people miserable has nothing to do with the retributive reason for worrying about it. We might as well speak of the common problem of circuses: the utilitarian problem being whether circuses are for the greatest happiness, and the retributive problem being whether anyone deserves to go. Or we could speak of the common problem of dinner, where the chef's problem is to serve up a tasty meal, and the diner's problem is to get to dinner on time. That a given situation worries people, whose reasons for being worried are not only different but are actually or potentially in conflict, is not sufficient ground for saying that those people have the same problem.

It might be argued that there are independent moral problems concerning punishment, abortion, experiments on animals, and so forth, on the ground that issues are presented concerning what practices we should follow and that there are different moral considerations pro and con that must be taken into account in arriving at a morally defensible decision. But what does it mean to say that a certain line of reasoning 'must' be taken into account or to say that a given decision is 'morally defensible'? Again, these are theory-dependent matters. The utilitarian need acknowledge no valid consideration that is not at bottom an appeal to the general happiness. The only morally defensible decisions, for the contractarian, are those that fall under supposedly agreed-upon (or hypothetically agreeable) principles.

The necessity to arrive at a common decision may be practical: where persons with different moral points of view, backed by firmly held theories, are at odds in incipiently chaotic ways—as, for example, over abortion—then there 'must' be a drive for consensus. But that is, of course, consequential reasoning. We can't escape the difficulty of the nonindependence of moral problems by promoting them to 'practical' problems; for practical problems are, in this context, problems only for persons who are concerned about consequences, who want, say, to minimize misery by the avoidance of a chaotic social life. If adherence to duty or prior agreement takes precedence over the avoidance of misery, then the supposed necessity to arrive at a common decision evaporates.

It might be argued, alternatively, that if moral problems could not be understood and stated in a theory-independent way, then we could hardly account for there being different moral theories about the most appropriate way to deal with them: that the very existence of different moral theories is evidence for the existence of independent moral problems. This is, of course, to beg the question. The question is whether the standard theories speak to the same issues or are merely contingently concerned about what is to be done or what practice is to be adopted—consequentialists being concerned about a problem of minimizing misery; Kantians, about the demands of duty; and so on.

I will not, I am sure, have convinced everyone that there is something amiss with the standard ethical theories, signaled by the dependence on their acceptance of what is to count as a moral problem. "Suppose," it might be said, "that by 'moral problems' we just mean problems concerning the general happiness (or duties, or contracts). Then there would be nothing indefensibly reductive about refusing to recognize as a moral problem what does not concern consequences (duties, contracts). Is this not analogous to refusing to recognize as a chemical problem what does not involve the chemical composition of things? Suppose that, without realizing it, by 'moral problem' we just mean 'problem concerned with the good or bad consequences of actions'?"

The difficulty with this move is analogous to the difficulty with claims about the meaning of moral terms, such as 'good'.[3] If the meaning of 'good' is, say, 'conducive to general happiness', then we can no longer use the word 'good' to commend the general happiness. Correspondingly, if what we mean by 'moral problem' is 'problem concerning the general happiness', then we cannot question whether moral problems *are* problems that concern the general happiness. We have put a definitional stop on a live philosophical question. There is nothing wrong with such a move if it is taken simply as a suggestion that we explore the possibility that there *is* an identity of meaning. But that there is not is pretty plain. In claiming that moral questions simply are questions about good consequences by virtue of meaning, we not only settle a large philosophical question by fiat, but we also rule out as moral questions what, as we shall see in a moment, is a very wide, rich, and varied set of questions that have strong claim to being moral.

If it is true that the only moral problems are consequential ones, this is a claim yet to be demonstrated; and it must be demonstrated in the face of what certainly appear to be potent counter examples. So it cannot be accepted as a sound argument, defending ethical theories against the charge that they determine what is a moral problem, that one of these theories is true.

What I have said thus far is intended to raise a question about the standard ethical theories. If they are not alternative ways of dealing with moral problems, then what are they supposed to do? I do not want to be understood as saying that there are no moral problems; quite the contrary. I want to say that the field of moral problems is so large and various that the narrow subfields picked out by ethical theories fail to include most of what they should include. But what, then, is to count as a moral problem; and how, without recourse to a standard ethical theory, is it possible to locate the field of moral problems?

Rather than beginning by building a form into which anything that is to count as a moral problem must fit, it may be useful to glance at the range of issues that, intuitively, we are willing to count as moral problems. Here we can do no more than glance; and we can do so without assuming that there must be common threads or family resemblances to be found among them. Some moral problems, as has often been recognized, have a quasi-legal character: they presuppose a network of rules, and they concern the rights, duties, responsibilities, liabilities, and obligations of those who fall under the rules. Immanuel Kant, Jean Piaget, R. S. Peters, R. M. Hare, and many other philosophers are tempted to incorporate all moral problems under this heading. This temptation leads, by easy steps, to the erection of an ethical theory that will then itself allow, as a moral problem, only what can be described in the appropriate quasi-legal language. Since this is a language that admits of very great extension (witness the radically different sorts of things that Ross brings together under 'prima facie duties'),[4] the range that it can be made to cover is large; but it is not large enough to incorporate, without questionable extensions of ordinary meaning, the sorts of issues to which we now turn. Let us begin, then, in a different way.

It can be a moral problem whether what I propose to do or approve would be

arrogant	presumptuous
calculating	selfish
cold	unfair
conscienceless	ungenerous
cowardly	ungrateful
cruel	unsympathetic
deceptive	untactful
disloyal	untruthful
dishonest	vindictive
intolerant	

It can be a moral problem what the benevolent thing to do or to approve is, in the circumstances, or the kind thing, the loyal thing, the honest thing, the just thing. In short, it can be a moral problem whether what I am considering doing or approving is consistent or not with the standards or ideals by which I would like to live.

We have, then, a very rich language for the assessments of persons, actions, policies, and practices—a language that is mostly relegated by contemporary theories to the region of 'virtue and vice', a region that is then set aside, never to be returned to. The terms of this language, when they are invoked, set the direction for subsequent discussion. We know what it is to argue the question of whether an action or practice is unjust, unkind, or deceptive. The charge or the intimation that it is one of these things requires an answer—a justification or an excuse for doing or for approving the act or the practice. It requires an answer to whatever extent we have common standards of justice, noncruelty, nondeceptiveness, and so on.

The standard theories, however, say, not what you or I should do or approve of in the light of our standards, but what anyone should do or approve of who falls under the description appropriate to the theory. The appropriate description, for the utilitarian, for example, is of a being who is in a position to affect the general happiness in one way or other. The agent as a part of the causal nexus is what counts, not the agent as a person who has standards and ideals. The standards and ideals of the agent in question are irrelevant to the discussion about what he or she should do. Kantian and contractarian ethics also determine what anyone should do—anyone, that is, who falls under the theoretically appropriate description, a description that sets aside ideals and standards as irrelevant, except insofar as they can be stated in the theoretical description.

But the agent may care if what he is doing is just, if it is loyal, if it is cowardly, kind, merely sentimental, or decent. He may worry that in acting or approving as he proposes, he would be negligent, vindictive, or intolerant. He may be asking, that is, not what anyone should do, but what, given the circumstances, *he* should do—whether the proposed action or practice would be worthy of him, would be consistent with his standards and ideals. He is concerned to know not just what would be incumbent on anyone but also what, if he did as he proposed, he should then be—what kind of person. What is incumbent on anyone is incumbent on him. But to confine his deliberation to duty, prior agreements, or possible consequences for the general happiness would be to leave out much of what concerns his status as a person who has standards and ideals that he does not necessarily prescribe for everyone.

It might be contended that while agents may, in the region of supererogation, set themselves standards beyond the requirements of moral duty, still these standards are not, strictly, a part of morality with which moral theory need concern itself; it should be enough that theory provide the underlying rationale of moral judgment. But how is 'underlying rationale' being used here? If the underlying rationale in question determines what is to count as a moral problem, then the question is begged as to how there can be independently recognizable moral problems according to the criteria set by the theory. But if the underlying rationale is understood, not as determining what is a moral problem, but as speaking only to the question of how to deal with moral problems, then it is not clear why questions of loyalty, kindness, concern, and honesty are pushed upstairs into a supererogatory, but not 'essentially moral', realm. It is not clear, anyway, that these considerations have to do with what is supererogatory. For there may be minimal as well as high standards of loyalty, kindness, and the rest. One should not be disloyal, cruel, unconcerned about others, or dishonest. These agent-directed, as opposed to merely act-directed, considerations are as legitimately a part of moral deliberation as are the considerations favored by ethical theories, considerations concerning what a morally anonymous 'anyone' should do.

S hall we be happy pluralists, then, reveling in the multiplicity of the modes of assessment? How can we be if we would bring order to moral judgment? The list of virtues and vices is lengthy, unordered, and theoretically amorphous. The items on it are of very different weights: presumptuousness is less serious than dishonesty; cruelty is worse than arrogance. Some items on the list are quite obviously relative to time and circumstance or to background beliefs about God, nature, and human nature. We cannot today accept as virtues the qualities prized by Christian anchorites such as Saint Simeon Stylites; Aristotle's High

Minded Man is, for us, faintly ludicrous. If ethics is to be more than the aesthetics of styles of life, it would seem that we must try to find or impose some form in or on our moral judgments. But it does not follow that we must search for universal principles applicable to every situation in which morally anonymous agents may find themselves. This grand aim may give way to the more modest one of trying to arrive at reasoned preferences among the standards we share, to find means for distinguishing between pseudo standards and ideals and genuine ones, and between standards that may be minimally expected of everyone and standards that go beyond a merely minimal morality.

A moral problem, then, is defined, not by the ethical theory that one holds, but by the standards and ideals that one has or shares: no standards or ideals, no problems. It concerns the range and interplay of these standards and ideals, their application to oneself and other persons, acts, practices, and institutions. Whoever is generally concerned about these matters is, on the present view, a student of ethics. He will be concerned with the nature and demands of justice, of loyalty, of honesty, of integrity, and of courage. He will worry about the relative weight of these very different sorts of considerations; but it will not be a part of his ambition to reduce all of them to one: to benevolence, say, or to conscientiousness or to honesty.

The difficulty with the standard theories that I have insisted upon is that one cannot make sense, independently of the theory adopted, of the claim that a given worry is a moral problem: that, from the point of view of the advocate of the theory, the only worries that are moral problems are those that arise for persons who accept the theory. All other supposed moral problems are merely illusory: they are not moral problems at all. But why can't this same difficulty be raised for the person who has reflectively accepted a certain pattern of standards and ideals? Won't he also say that whoever does not accept that pattern or whoever accepts some alternative pattern is deceived about what constitutes a moral problem? Won't the pattern that he accepts determine what is to count as a moral problem as surely as does the standard theory?

The answer, as might be expected, is a forthright 'yes' and 'no', combined with an 'it depends' and a 'does it matter?'

Some minimal public standards we not only hold but think that everyone should hold. These standards have to do, largely, with public order and the achievement of common goals. Often these minimal public standards are expressed in the quasi-legal language, mentioned above: the language of rights, duties, obligations, and so on. To the extent that we are willing to confine the field of moral problems to conflicts within this quasi-legal network and, possibly, to conflicts between what one is inclined to do and what the network demands of us, we can say that whatever is a moral problem is a problem about the application of rights, duties, and so on, to particular cases. What is more, we will say that this network applies to everyone, even though, on reflection, we will admit that the farther out the network spreads over the cultures of distant peoples, the more attenuated it becomes. But it is difficult to imagine a person the whole of whose pattern of standards and ideals is confined to minimal public standards. To say nothing more, he would be forced to abandon all of the modes of assessment of persons, acts, and practices iterated above. Only if he were willing to declare that the minimal standards, under the quasi-legal network, were the only moral standards would he confine moral problems to problems about or under those standards. Such a person would have, if not a reductive ethical theory, at least the next stage to one. For he would, by hypothesis, have an account, perhaps so far insufficiently general, of what is fundamental in moral judgment, an account that is to be applied universally.

Nearly everyone's—arguably everyone's—patterns of standards and ideals extend well beyond the minimal public standards. Many people, for example, are in some respects Stoics. They value acts and attitudes that foster or protect peace of mind, a kind of self-sufficiency that is impervious to the unhappy vicissitudes of the external world, even including the vicissitudes of their own bodies; and they correspondingly disvalue things that are not enough under the control of their will: luxuries, riches, popularity, and acclaim. They cultivate their powers of concentration, abstention, and control of their feelings. For them, fortitude, pride, and self-control are leading virtues; humility, meekness, and sentimentality are vices. Not only do they cultivate the virtues in themselves and do what they can to extirpate the vices, but they also try to do the same for their children, to encourage virtue in those about whom they care, and to admire these qualities wherever they appear.

But the notion that this pattern of approved and disapproved qualities is a universal touchstone of moral judgment would seem to them out of place. The stoical pattern is but one pattern; and the Stoic is likely to recognize that even though it would be nice if everyone were stoical, it is not what is to be expected. It is in fact an element of pride that he lives by a code that is not adhered to, or even appreciated, by most people. People who do not appreciate the pattern are likely, at the Stoic's worst, to be depreciated by him as servile, slaves of inclination, courters of popularity, and generally weak. But at his best, the Stoic will recognize that the non-Stoic may be something other than morally flabby. He may hold to a different pattern of ideals and standards. For example, he may place a lot of weight on sympathy, fellow feeling, and universal love.

In short, it is not a necessary consequence of his acceptance of the Stoic pattern of ideals and standards that the only moral problems are those that are problems for him as a Stoic or that Stoicism is the only avenue to the recognition of the moral landscape. It is not inconsistent for him to recognize that non-Stoics may have moral problems too. He may recognize, as the theorist may not, that there are problems that would be approached in one way by him and in another way by a Christian. But for the theorist, no analogous recognition is possible. There are no problems 'outside of' the theory.[5]

One additional matter should be mentioned. There are two very *general* theories of ethics that claim to cover the field of moral problems: consequentialism and formalism. Consequential theories hold that the moral acceptability of actions, policies, or practices is determined by the consequences of doing the actions or of adopting the policies or practices. Morally acceptable acts, and so forth, are acts, and so forth, that generate the best possible balance of good over bad consequences. That is the general form of the theory. Of course, the consequentialist must then go on to tell us something about how we are to distinguish good from bad consequences; he then becomes a consequentialist of this or that kind, the best-known kind being classical utilitarianism. Formalistic theories hold that the moral acceptability of actions, and so forth, is determined by the mere consistency of that action, and so forth, with a set of general rules that are held to apply to everyone. That is the general form of *that* theory. The formalist may then go on to specify some particular rules with which other rules must then be made consistent. These are typically rules of a very high order of generality, such as Kant's rule that everyone is to be treated as an end and never merely as a means.

Given the most general and the particular forms of these two theories, we may notice an ambivalence in their possible responses to the charge I have made that there is something fishy about a theory that purports to resolve moral problems, when at the same time it determines what is and is not a moral problem. Let us, for example, take the general form of consequentialism and contrast it with classical utilitarianism. In the general form, *any* problem concerning what ought to be done or about what policy or practice to adopt is a moral problem, since any policy may be evaluated by its good or bad consequences. There is not, thus, on the general form of the theory, any way of distinguishing moral problems from practical problems, if a practical problem is simply a problem about what to do or about what policy or practice to adopt. The general consequentialist might respond, to the objection that the theory determines what is a problem, that general consequentialism is, in this respect, unharmful. It is unharmful because, since moral problems are coextensive with practical ones, it cannot exclude as a moral problem any set of problems that would be recognized by any other theory.

However, there is no one who is content to stay at the level of generality in question, since it makes sense to demand of the consequentialist what *sort* of consequences he is willing to count as good. Once he specifies, as the classical utilitarians do, he then does exclude as moral problems what others might well want to count as moral problems and does include as moral problems what others might not accept as such.

If we do not bear in mind the distinction between the general and the specific forms of the two theories in question, we are likely to miss the force of the criticism upon which I have been insisting. For if we have the general form of the theory in mind, we will not be conscious of the role of theory in determining what is a moral problem. The two theories, in their general form, range over the same set of problems—all practical problems. But of course, the consequentialist's reason for calling a particular problem a moral one will at the same time be different from, and inconsistent with, the formalist's reason. This will not matter at the general level. But neither theory can be merely general; the theorist must specify the sort of consequence or the particular principle he has in mind, on pain of providing no criterion for distinguishing acceptable from unacceptable acts, and so forth. Once specification is offered, the arbitrariness of the theory can be made evident by ranges of counter examples of moral problems that are not covered by the specific kind of consequence or principle.

For the teaching of ethics, what are the implications of the point that, for the standard ethical theories, there are no common moral problems? I would suggest at least two. First, we should be explicit that in accepting a theory, the student is accepting a certain account not only of how to deal with moral problems but also of what a moral problem is. Second, we should consider shifting the focus of ethics off a too-exclusive concern with problematics and should look again at the tradition that takes qualities of character to be the center of the subject.

The attitude of most moral philosophers toward the courses they teach in introductory ethics is, I think, ambivalent. On the one hand, they are likely to say that a clear distinction must be made between the study of ethics and the inculcation of moral belief; that we study ethics just to clear our heads of a lot of misleading notions, conceptual confusions, and bad arguments; that it is in this sense only that the student is morally better off for having studied the subject; and that to the extent that moral judgment requires a clear head, ethics is a help. On the other hand, teachers of ethics are prone to offer the standard theories as so many normative alternatives that the student can choose between as his basis for making judgments about particular cases. It is on this latter basis that teachers can reassure themselves that they are doing something useful—they are providing the student with the means of discovering whether he is a consequentialist, a Kantian, or whatever. Indeed, such discoveries are made: some students find Kant, Mill, or some other writer bringing into focus what they had only vaguely thought. But even though Kant may bring to focus what was vague, it is wrong to present Kantian ethics as an alternative mode of resolving moral problems—problems that are waiting there for an adequate resolving theory. To be a Kantian is to hold to criteria that determine what is to count as a moral problem, not just to provide means for approaching moral problems.

Conceptual analysis and confusion clearing, on the other hand, are not methodologically tied to the presentation of and to the argument for ethical theories. The analyst can also devote his attention to the distinctions between justification and excuse, between excuses such as infancy and excuses such as mistake, between mistake and accident, shame and guilt, is and ought, reason and cause, and so on. This is to say nothing of the theoretically ignored modes of assessment of persons, actions, and policies that are enshrined in language. For to say of a person, act, or policy that he or it is unjust is to open a form of discussion that has its own rules of relevance and permitted moves. The same can be said of benevolence, helpfulness, honesty, kindness, sensitivity, and on and on.

If different persons weigh these modes differently and incorporate different but overlapping modes in their moral pantheons, this is not cause for despair in the teaching of ethics. For the moral philosopher can then seek to discover the reasons for preferring one moral configuration to another and to present alternative patterns of the moral life, not as alternative modes for the resolution of problems, but in the interest of heightening the student's understanding of the nature and relative defensibility or indefensibility of the large choices that he must make. But the philosopher is ill advised, I have been arguing, to present these large alternatives as so many mutually exclusive criteria of what is to count as being of moral concern.

There is a defense of the standard ethical theories that I have not considered, that has not to my knowledge been offered, and that may hold promise of meeting the objection I have been raising—the objection that there are no theory-independent criteria of a moral problem and that the standard theories offer an inadequate account of the moral agent and his motivations and interests. This is to claim that even though standard theories may seem to curtail the range of and to oversimplify moral problems and to offer an abstract view of the moral agent, these seeming disadvantages are really advantages, in the quest for defensible moral decisions. This can be appreciated, it might be argued, by thinking of the theories as *models* of moral thought and discourse.⁶ It might be said that models such as electronic models of nerve networks may provide illuminating analogies with what is being modeled. We may find many positive analogies that we had not expected to find or had not seen when we first constructed the model. We may actually learn about the behavior of nerve networks from the formally neat computer model and see relationships that were not apparent in nature. Similarly, it could be contended, utilitarian or Kantian or contractarian theory can serve as models of moral reflection and discourse. We can use the theories not only to sharpen moral reasoning, to make it more precise, but also to illuminate moral reflection, to reveal aspects of moral problems that in the absence of the model we would not have appreciated.

The notion that the standard theories are best understood as models of moral discourse would seem to require that we set off from other conceptions the particular conception of 'model' that is most relevant to the purpose and that we explore the question whether a normative theory can count as a model.

The answer to the latter question must, again, be yes and no. Yes if we focus on the formalizing character of the theory, when the theory is considered as a kind of ordered, smoothed analogue of moral discourse. No when we consider the function the standard ethical theories are usually supposed to have, as modes of resolution of moral problems. To think of theories as modes of resolution is to do worse than ignore the presence of disanalogies between theoretical and moral discourse. It is to confuse theoretical premises and conclusions with the premises and conclusions of which they are analogues. It is to accept the universalized conclusion that follows from the theory as the conclusion sought by the moral agent in the light of the facts, standards, and ideals that give rise to the problem.

The notion that the standard moral theories are models of moral discourse is at once weaker and more defensible than the claim usually made or implied by theorists, that what is morally essential in moral discourse is captured by the theory. Unless a realist position with respect to the model be assumed, we can think of the model as a potentially useful *device* for understanding moral discourse. This is the sort of view that is usually taken of deontic logic. But to make this sort of claim for moral theories is certainly to claim far less than the utilitarians, the Kantians, and the contractarians ordinarily do. It is, at any rate, a topic worth pursuing.

4

The Justificatory Powers of the Standard Theories

Suppose that, for the sake of argument, we set aside the worry of chapter 3—that the standard ethical theories are relevant to moral problems only because they determine what counts as a moral problem. The question that remains is *how* the theory is supposed to be relevant.

Ethical theories are commonly supposed to have justificatory powers, to provide alternative ways of showing what is right or wrong, good or bad. If someone has doubts about what to do or approve, theory is ideally not merely helpful but also authoritative. It can guide us firmly to the right answer, and we can rely on its verdict, barring factual uncertainties and mistakes of logic, because it starts from principles that we may accept as unshakeable. They are, we may say, truisms: to deny them would be in some way absurd or even impossible. What this usually amounts to is that no one who wishes to deny them can at the same time be 'rational' or 'moral'. That is the line that the theorist typically takes against the skeptic. The skeptic is shown to be questioning what must be accepted by persons whose acceptance or denial counts, or has weight. But if he continues to question a truism, then his doubts may safely be ignored.

What concerns me here is not that there are no moral truisms but that given a list of them, it is no longer clear why the standard ethical theories are entitled to special status as justifiers of moral conclusions. It is not clear how we have advanced by adopting the theory.

I should like to thank Alvin Goldman, Robert Simon, and Christopher Gill for their criticisms of this chapter.

Here are some moral truisms: what is cruel, unjust, dishonest, selfish, or vindictive is, so far, morally unacceptable or undesirable.

No one whose opinion we respect seriously denies that cruelty is wrong, even if all or most of us are sometimes or even often cruel. The cruel person does not argue that cruelty is right; he argues that there are special circumstances that excuse or justify him in being cruel or that what appears to be cruel in his or others' behavior is not really so.

If it is a truism that cruelty is wrong, then that proposition (or expression of commitment) does not require justification. Where is justification to end but in truisms? But then, how are we to understand the relation between justificatory ethical theories and these truisms? Do the theories claim to justify the truisms? But how can a truism be justified? Are the truisms from which the theoretical justifications start in some way more fundamental than these truisms? How can that be?

Theoretical truisms are not more evidently true in the sense that they cannot be questioned by an earnest skeptic. He can question the principle of utility as readily as he can question the principle that cruelty is bad. They are not more evidently true in the sense that they are better proof against the relativism of time and culture. Contractarian justifications would not work in every culture. Kantians would not easily be understood in ancient Greece. So it is not clear how we have provided a foundation or a touchstone in introducing a means of supposedly justifying the list of truisms with which we began. Why not, then, end the quest for justification there?

The first objection to leaving it there that comes to mind is the sort that one may feel on reading W. D. Ross.[1] It is just not intellectually very satisfactory to answer the question of how we can justify our moral claims with a list of what Ross calls prima facie duties. There ought, it seems, to be some order. Some of the items on the list should be ranked as cases under others; there ought to be a way of determining not only the internal order but also the range of the list as well. Where does it end? How many prima facie duties are there? The second, a related, objection that may come to mind is that we are at too low a level of abstraction. What is wanted is a common characteristic of morally acceptable actions, policies, and so forth. What we are given is a set of characteristics, with no table of instructions indicating how they are to be related to one another. It is not terribly helpful, it may be felt, to be told that for an action, and so on, to be morally acceptable it must be just or kind or—whatever. Finally, what we want of a theory is that it give us a formula for determining what to do; but this theory does not do that either. It tells us that there is a list of considerations that must be taken into account in deciding. We should not do what is cruel, unjust, dishonest, and so forth. But we may, for all of that, be left undecided. Or we may decide, but not with the assurance that our decision is the certifiably right one, an assurance that we might have if we were armed with a theory.

On the other hand, the defense of Ross has always been that despite the intellectual unsatisfactoriness, the lack of certifiable answers for particular cases, still the analysis of moral justification that Ross offers has the advantage over all of its rivals that it is *candid*. Perhaps there is no conclusive way to provide the answer to particular moral difficulties. Perhaps that is just the nature of the case. Perhaps its being the nature of the case gives to moral discourse some of the characteristics that it has. There are, for example, no moral experts, as there should be if there were a theory from which decisions and particular cases could be deduced. But some people are wiser than others and deliberate more carefully. Perhaps there just are always decisions to be made. Perhaps adopting a theory won't make them in advance. Perhaps those decisions are the responsibility of the person who makes them, in the sense that in the end they determine his character.

I t is a mistake to look below bedrock for bedrock. But how to show that an appeal to justice or kindness or honesty is bedrock? How to convince the skeptic that it is so? Here we are faced, as the theorist is, with the problem of what is to count as *moral* skepticism. Can that be distinguished from general philosophical skepticism? The philosophical skeptic can doubt nearly anything. He can doubt that what seems to be a truism is true wherever the truism appears. But what, without losing his claim to attention or even his status as moral, can the moral skeptic doubt? Is he still a moral, as opposed to a philosophical, skeptic when he doubts that cruelty is a bad thing?

Why cannot a moral skeptic doubt that all of the so-called moral truisms are true? But that is moving too fast. We must first consider the person who doubts that one of them is true. He is supposed to doubt, for example, that those things that are cruel are bad. He might hold that cruelty is the way of the world and that whatever is, is instituted by God and is therefore right.[2] How can such a person be convinced of the truistic status of the claim made for cruelty? Well, what truisms does he accept? Does he accept, for example, that dishonesty or injustice are bad? Then why can we not argue that to be cruel is to initiate a situation in which injustice is a likely consequence? Or argue that cruelty is itself a form of injustice, given normal expectations of just treatment? In general, is it not fair to ask the skeptic about moral claims just which claims he is skeptical about and which he accepts? Can we not then try to show that the accepted considerations presuppose those that he rejects and thus build a network of justification through a process that moves laterally rather than vertically? Such a network would move from moral truth to moral truth, rather than from all claims about right and wrong to one moral truism.[3]

But what if the skeptic rejects all moral truisms; what if he demands a proof for all of them together, for the whole network of truisms? Then what is there to say? If we cannot go back to a truism, where is there to go? We have no purchase on the subject. We must now determine if the skepticism of moral claims amounts to uncertainty about them or to rejection of them—that is, if it is more than philosophical. If it is, we must flag the skeptic as a person who may be unamenable to moral reasons or even as a person whom we must be wary of and must warn others about.

One source of the notion that there must be a general and abstract theoretical justification available to warrant all moral claims is that in our talk about moral duties and obligations and rights, we have the idea that what we are delineating is a coherent structure, something quite real. The question of whether I have a duty or obligation or a right seems to look to a two-position answer—yes or no. At least it seems that there are two-position answers in the clear cases. There must be cases in which these claims are warrantable, conclusively demonstrable. The analogy with law is again at work, and it may be felt that the analogy is an appropriate one. Why should we not have a nonlegal set of rules couched in language that laps over from law, a set of rules that can be delineated by a patient anthropologist? But if there is such a set and if moral claims can be couched in the appropriate language, is it not necessary to ask what justifies the whole set together? Why should we not accept code A in preference to code B, even when B is the current code? Talk about honesty and kindness will not tell us which moral code is morally justifiable. But that is something we must know if we are to make sound moral judgments.

Again, is it not fair to ask the skeptic *which* claims about duties, rights, or obligations he has doubts about? And if it is about a particular claim concerning rights, is it not fair to try to show that the existence of that right follows from the truth of certain statements about duties and obligations or about other rights? But if the skeptic's wish is to question the whole network of claims concerning rights, and so forth, what are we to say? Are we not then justified in giving no weight to his doubts or in putting ourselves and others on guard against him?

Of course, like the skeptic about the network of justice, courage, kindness, and so on, the skepticism may be philosophical. It may have no practical import. The skeptic may be quite content to live under or by the code, but at the same time he would feel more comfortable, or intellectually better satisfied, if he knew an argument to show why the particular code under which he lives is defensible. But then (to enter the circle again), defensible against what doubts? What, in particular, about the code is it that bothers him and for what reason? If it is about the code as a whole, then where are we to begin, if we cannot appeal to rights, duties, or obligations in its defense?

There is another move in the antiskeptical argument, a move suggested by the two divisions of moral discourse mentioned above: the sort of discourse having to do with virtue truisms and that having to do with code truisms. One could go a certain distance with the contention that code truisms rest on virtue truisms. The usual argument for codes, as well as for basic rights and obligations, is a Hobbesian one: that in their absence, life would be somewhere beyond miserable. A different sort of argument is that codes provide the context in which honesty, loyalty, justice, and kindness, say, are possible. To whatever extent we value these qualities of persons and common life, we will value the conditions that make them possible. Some codes (nondiscriminatory ones, say) provide a more secure ground for the development of these qualities than do other codes; hence the former are morally preferable.

The difference between this sort of a justification and a Hobbesian one might best be captured by speaking of considerations that are internal or external to morality.[4] Considerations having to do with the provision of a platform for the development of the virtues are appealing only to persons who already value the virtues. They are, in this sense, internal. The considerations adduced by Hobbes are only contingently, or externally, related to moral concerns. In Hobbesian thought, the state of nature, if allowed to continue, is likely to lead to cruelty. But our motivation, when entering the contract and thereafter, is the self-interested one of avoiding the misery that general cruelty is likely to cause us. If we could somehow, in a qualified state of nature, protect ourselves against cruelty and the other miseries endured by everyone else, then we would have no motive to try to get out of the state of nature. The motivation of the friend of the virtues would be otherwise; it would be a moral one.

We can contrast having an ethical theory that supposedly justifies particular moral claims in a highly structured and abstract way, as the standard theories want to do, with insisting upon a certain set of moral considerations as aids to reflection and in the interest of justification. The former, the theoretical, approach may be motivated in part by the feeling that if there were more than one way of supporting a moral claim, there could be more than one valid moral opinion about the merits of the claim. And this would be insupportable. It would be insupportable because, it could be thought, a moral theory must tell us what to do. It cannot tell that to us if we must still decide what to do after the theory has yielded its verdict but another theory has yielded an incompatible verdict. A moral theory can tolerate arguments about what to do that rest on the interpretation of the available facts, but it cannot accept that there may be equally valid, but in principle inconsistent, versions of the correct answer. Thus, a utilitarian can accept that when the facts are in, utilitarians may still differ on what is conducive to the greatest happiness, but he cannot accept that there should be a validly drawn conclusion concerning what to do that rests on some nonutilitarian mode of argument.

Yet the recognition of alternative types of consideration does not constitute a surrender to relativism. The resultant decision is not necessarily irrational or arbitrary. The modes of discussion are neither reducible to nor subsumable under one another. They are simply different modes—related, but different. To defend a course of action on the ground that it is just is to open a discussion to which questions of kindness or gratitude are irrelevant—not irrelevant to the question of what to do but irrelevant to the question of whether the course of action is just. It can be just and unkind or cruel and just, and we can have a right to do it, even though to do it would be selfish or disloyal. To do it might be disloyal to A but loyal to B, dishonest in our relations with C, and unkind to D. We will just have to *decide*. The questions of whether something is cruel or unjust or dishonest or disloyal or selfish or vindictive or overbearing or intemperate are simply different questions. All of them have claim to be moral. To raise and discuss them is to enter into different modes of moral discourse, modes that are different from each other and from the modes inaugurated by equally valid claims concerning rights, right, duty, and obligation.

The burden of proof is on whoever would reduce all of these modes of discussion to one mode through the adoption of a theory. The decision that results from taking all of these modes into account is not a sum or a deductive conclusion. It is a verdict, a judgment. But the judgment's not following from the premises as a necessary consequence does not make it less justifiable. It rests on moral truisms, and it has not a chance of resting more securely than that.

No one can, by accepting a moral theory, avoid the responsibility for making particular decisions. We can't judge the moral character of a person by learning what theory he subscribes to. The character develops and is revealed, even to the agent, in the course of deliberating and deciding. If he allows weight to honesty, he is to that extent moral; and so on for justice, and so forth. If he could make one theoretical decision and could ever afterward calculate what follows from that decision for the present case, then his conclusions concerning particular cases would be testimony not so much to his character as to his consistency.

It does not follow, however, that because we must make decisions over and over, we must do so in a moral vacuum. Our decisions are not arbitrary in any damaging sense. We must balance justice against justice, against kindness, against honesty, and so on. And we must then consider what to do. Given overall concern for others, our moral judgment will consist in the sensitivity and care with which we weigh these considerations against one another. The decisions will be arbitrary only in the sense that we may have simply to choose between alternatives for which there are equally compelling arguments. That is morally defensible arbitrariness.

Against the argument of this chapter—that theoretical truisms have no greater claim to justificatory powers than appeals to justice, honesty, and so forth—the objection could be raised that the standard ethical theories do not necessarily *rest on* truisms. It might be contended that theories are structures of a different sort. Rather than resting on moral truisms, they provide a framework for understanding them. Thus, the utilitarian theory, for example, constitutes an attempt to reconcile the truisms that we do accept and to provide a test for the acceptability of purported truisms. It is not so much truism based as truism organizing.

It is a rationale for the canon of truisms that are such, but not for other purported truisms.

The objection fails to meet the criticism on two counts. First, it fails to specify in what respects the supposed 'structures for understanding' truisms are not themselves presented as truisms. Both Mill and Bentham concede that it is impossible to prove the principle of utility; only 'considerations capable of determining the understanding' can be offered. Why is this so? Is it not that when once we grasp the principle of utility, we supposedly see, or understand, that this is the fundamental principle of ethics? What is the force of the first section of the *Foundations of the Metaphysics of Morals?* Is it not that we are led to recognize that there is a germ of truth in the common understanding of morals and that once this germ is revealed to us clearly, it must be acknowledged as true beyond question? Does not contract theory rest on the truism that agreements that are freely made, in good faith, must be kept?

Secondly, the objection does not stop, as it should, over the distinction between the explanatory and the justificatory claims that can be made for a theory. What is at issue here is whether the standard ethical theories actually have the justificatory powers that they are claimed to have. It is quite possible that they might provide the structures within which it is easier to understand what does and does not justify a moral judgment without at the same time adding any justificatory force to those judgments. This is a large topic to broach here, and I can do no more than throw out a suggestion that seems to me to be worthy of further thought. Why not think of the utilitarian theory, for example, as a model within which a translation can be found for all of the considerations we regard, intuitively, as having weight—a model that can serve as a calculating device that will make optimum use of those considerations, when they are taken together? An interpretation of theories of this kind would give them the sort of function that mathematical formulae have in dealing with problems that are capable of mathematical formulation. But it does not follow that because we can find a place for all of our intuitively acceptable judgments in such a theory, we should start *from* the theory in determining whether our judgments are justified. The the-

ory, in its explanatory function, takes the intuitively acceptable judgments as given. It does not provide them with a
foundation. For it to do that, we would have to suppose that
it provides us with some truth that is more trustworthy than
the truism that cruelty is wrong.

Another sort of objection is that 'cruelty is wrong' is
truistic only because it is tautologous. It is tautologous in the
same way that 'murder is wrong' is. Since 'murder' means
wrongful killing, we can't deny the wrongfulness of murder
without contradiction. But it does not follow from the
meaning of 'cruelty', 'dishonesty', 'ungratefulness', or 'disloyalty' that those dispositions or the actions that are evidences of them are wrong. Cruelty, for example, can be
defined as taking pleasure in bringing about the suffering of
other persons or sensate creatures. While a definition of this
kind needs refinement, it is enough to show that a neutral
definition is possible. There is, then, no contradiction in
saying that cruelty is not wrong.

How do we know what is and is not a moral truism? How
do we know that cruelty is wrong and that honesty is
right? If we cannot say how to draw the line between truisms
and morally debatable claims, then how can we rest such
confidence on the supposed truisms? Is the claim that cruelty
is wrong beyond criticism? Yes and no.

Yes: It is what we may expect others to recognize. It
should be enough to give pause that a proposed line of
action would be cruel. If it does not give pause, then
something is amiss. The hearer has not heard or has not
understood or does not believe what is being said. But if he
has heard and understood and if he does believe that what
he is about to do would be cruel, then, prima facie, he ought
not do it; and he should realize that if he does do it, there
must be a strong-enough countervailing moral reason. What
is strong enough he will have to decide; and in deciding, he
will define his character. But as a moral person, he will not
doubt that cruelty is wrong.

No: It is not beyond criticism. We may not easily
understand how someone could question it, have doubts
about it, or what the grounds are on which he would argue

that we may be cruel. It is inconceivable that a moral being would question it. But someone may not yet be fully moral. It is conceivable that we would have to make clear to him the wrongness of cruelty. After all, we do this for children. They may have to be taught that to tie a can to a dog's tail is cruel, that continually to remind Johnny of his ignominious defeat at the hands of Billy is cruel, and so on. We do not so much teach him that this or that is cruel and that what is cruel is wrong as we teach him that this or that is cruel-wrong, unjust-wrong, disloyal-wrong, and so on. What he learns is that there are different sorts of wrong and different character traits that he had best not acquire.

But if an adult who is otherwise psychologically normal does not recognize the wrongness of cruelty, how can we show him that it is wrong? Are there good reasons by which we can persuade him that he should not be cruel? This is a touchy question, because if he does not recognize the wrongness of cruelty, we will not be at all sure of what he will recognize in the way of a moral consideration or argument. We will have to cast around. Is he amenable to any other moral considerations? Can we argue from justice? Can we show him that given similar circumstances, he might, under poetic justice, be treated in the same way? Can we appeal to his sense that others are as sensitive and as full of feeling as he is? Is his attitude toward cruelty an adamant refusal to recognize its wrongness or simply an inability to recognize its wrongness?

The *range* of moral considerations becomes an issue in reflecting on the possibility that someone may not recognize the wrongness of cruelty. He may recognize that he should not be cruel to humans but fail to recognize that he should not be cruel to other sensitive beings; or perhaps he thinks that he may be cruel to Jews but not to other gentiles. Or he may think that cruelty to debtors or sinners or witches or whatever is fine, but not to friends and relatives. But of course, this is easier to handle. We can argue that what he had thought were exclusive classes can overlap, such as the classes of friends and sinners, or the classes of Jews and relatives. Or we can argue that he may himself fall into one of those classes. Or we may argue that sinners and slaves have, in common with friends and relatives, the morally crucial quality that they are sensitive and can suffer. But after all, this is not the sort of person who concerns us so much as does the person who simply denies that what is cruel is morally wrong. That is the limiting case, the case that is nearly inconceivable, the case in which we have to grope for what we would or could say, supposing that reasoning, as opposed to therapy, is what is appropriate.

Suppose the person is the bearer of a culture in which cruelty is the norm, in which people are expected to be cruel to one another. We would first have to be sure that this is not a case of limited range, as above. It is hard to conceive of a culture in which it is taken for granted that anyone may be cruel to anyone; the boundaries of what is to count as a culture are strained. Could such a collection of people have a common culture?—a question somewhere between empirical and conceptual. For the sake of argument, suppose that it is the norm that anyone may be cruel to anyone and that the culture still somehow coheres as a culture. What then are we to say to the bearer of such a culture? Is there anything that we can say? Is his belief that cruelty is generally permissible or perhaps even desirable a count, a fatal count, against the thesis that the wrongness of cruelty is a moral truism?

Much of what we can say to the person who believes that cruelty is permissible would, strictly, be morally irrelevant. It is irrelevant to appeal covertly to his self-interest in avoiding pain; but that is what we could be doing in appealing to justice, if the appeal to justice is understood as a warning of what might likely happen to him if the circumstances were reversed. That should not be the point of bringing up justice. Rather, the objective is to make him *realize* the wrongness of cruelty. He might otherwise avoid cruelty only in those circumstances and societies in which poetic justice to the cruel person is likely. But that is not the mark of a moral person. He must not be cruel *because of what cruelty to other persons is,* because he is purposely making them suffer unnecessarily. That is what he should never allow himself to do, even though he will often be tempted to do it. The point of the position-reversing arguments from justice is to bring this home to him. That is why imagination—the capacity to see or understand what it would be like to be the person who is suffering cruelty—is the moral point.[5] It is not that *he* might suffer cruelty if poetic justice prevails. If he were as immune as Gyges to the machinations of others, still he might be brought to imagine what it is like to suffer cruelty and then just to see that, given that it is like *that*, one should not inflict cruelty; one should not be cruel.

Cruelty may have to be identified for him. He may not have realized that he *is* cruel, that that is a concept, that there is such a concept, which captures the way that he is to other persons. This makes sense in the moral education of children. They may not realize that there is this way of being that they must recognize and try to control in themselves. They cannot understand that they are cruel and that that is wrong before they have recognized that cruelty *exists* and that it is something that one can fall into.

The wrongness of cruelty is not a *doctrine* for which good reasons can be adduced, even though we may be able, by relating it to justice, to adduce reasons; for then it would be, in principle, possible to refute the doctrine. But that cruelty is wrong is not up for debate. It is something learned in training that brings us to the position where we can recognize moral issues and can debate them. Failure to recognize the wrongness of cruelty is prima facie evidence of a flaw of character, rather than of doctrinal error.

One should do one's duty, attend to one's obligations, and respect rights; one should take care what consequences will likely follow from an action or a line of action; one should respect contracts. But none of this is morally more central than being just, avoiding cruelty, and being honest are central. My question is why moral philosophers should suppose that in order to justify moral claims, it is necessary or desirable to move from 'the central point' to those that are 'less central'. We do not do our duty because it is duty; we do it because it is what, depending on the sort of duty it is, we must do if we are to be just, honest, properly grateful, and so on. We must pay attention to consequences because we want to know what it is that we are bringing about—a necessary condition of knowing if what we are doing is morally defensible. Classical utilitarians are right to be concerned with the effects that our actions and policies may have on others; they are perverse in limiting that concern to the happiness of others.

Perversity gets wide scope because of the elasticity of the languages of duty and consequence as modes of discourse within which much of what we want to talk about can be cast. It is something like the language of numbers. So much can be captured by numbers, given a numerical value, that we are apt to think, as we become addicted to number talk, that only what can be captured need be taken into account. But there are regions in which the numerical mode is misleading, in that it leads us away from what ought to be at issue. It takes us away, not only by winnowing out what cannot be numerically expressed, but also by raising issues of numerical interpretation that would not have been raised at all had the numerical mode been more modestly confined to regions in which it is obviously relevant.

The utilitarian or Kantian may well be impatient with this analogy. If he is a forthright and sufficiently unqualified adherent of his doctrine, he will be convinced that the introduction of the favored mode of talk, so far from being a diversion from what is central, is just the identification of what is central and, by the same token, of what is peripheral. It is the vision that morality is a kind of law or that it really is concerned with the general happiness that, so he believes, cuts through the fog of moral discourse and lends it the clear outlines, the unity, that it must have.

But the unity of moral discourse as thus given, by the discovery of what is supposedly fundamental, is a spurious unity, founded on a mistaken discovery. For, in the clutch, the legal analogue and the consequential one have to give way to appeals to honesty, justice, trustworthiness, noncruelty, and so on. These appeals are central in the sense that if a person is unable to recognize their force, then his opinions on moral matters carry no weight. But a person may deliberate on and off for a lifetime about moral matters, to good effect, and not be captured by either the legal or the consequential models of moral discourse. He may not need the kind of unity that they can impart to his thought. They could even mislead him into thinking that until some fundamental principle of law or teleology is found, there is no possibility of finding solid ground for his decisions.

W hy is it that anyone would suppose that there should be a single item, ultimately, on the list of considerations that can justify moral claims? Why suppose that a satisfactory theory is one that yields determinate answers to the question of whether or not one should enter into a line of action?

I am aware of only one argument that there should be but one governing sort of moral consideration: it is the one offered by John Stuart Mill in the last chapter of *A System of Logic.*[6] Mill contends that if there were more than one principle, we could arrive at conflicting results for any proposed course of action. This, he takes it, without further argument, would be a theoretically unacceptable result. But what is wrong with the supposedly unacceptable result? Why should we not be willing to accept that there may be conflicting but equally valid moral views about what to do in some cases? Notice that Mill can countenance indecision brought about by a balancing-out of consequences for good or bad or for alternative lines of action between equally good consequences that are likely to ensue. But what he cannot accept is that there should be the indecisive result of moral deliberation that obtains from different sorts of fundamental considerations' having equal purchase. That is, however, the kind of indecisiveness that results in the agent's making a choice that defines his developing character, unlike the utilitarian's confident reapplication of a principle that is already accepted and ready-to-hand.

Perhaps the antipathy to a more candid appeal to the moral truisms that give weight to moral conclusions, as well as the preference for a theory that seems to offer unitary support for well-founded conclusions, is attributable to the wish to make sense of a world in which there are moral tensions. We must do what we can to combat ambiguity, to end vagueness in moral thought. There is enough confusion in the world already; ethical inquiry should not sanctify it, but should combat it. In the name of reason, ethical inquiry should cut through to what is at the bottom of all moral judgment. Of course, all of this supposes that there is *a* bottom, rather than bottoms; but it is worth trying more closely to understand.

There is such a thing as moral leadership; there are moral prophets and models. Moral leaders may bring us to see vividly again what we had lost sight of, to transform ourselves as we move progressively into a 'new' moral world. This can be said of great reformers in the public world who were as different as Bentham and Gandhi, or of those in the private world who were as different as Kierkegaard and Thoreau.

It is a characteristic of moral leaders that they convey to others what is 'supremely important', what 'weighs most', what transforms the moral vision of their time and of other times as well. What suddenly clarifies vision is not some new discovery. What now has great weight in deliberation tends to have been there all along. There is little that is really new in the moral world. The nature of the discovery is, rather, that something vitally important has been overlooked: that what is 'above all' important, as we had not been aware, is that we should be just or that we should be conscientious or that we should be pure in intention. Or that we should make ourselves instruments for the good of mankind or for the good of the kingdom of God on earth. Or that serenity matters most or that our concern should extend even to insentient creatures or that it should come to focus on the development of face-to-face communities. Or that relations with God matter most or that all men are brothers. Or that pride or lust or acquisitiveness is the root of evil and that moral goodness consists in rooting them out.

One sort of consideration then assumes transcendental importance in the thought of the moral leader and of his followers. It then may seem as if all of the other sorts of consideration, if they are worthy of attention, must be subsumed under the transcendent one. To bring them to attention, to insist on their weight against what is transcendent, can seem morally obtuse or recalcitrant or mindlessly conservative. The moral leader is, after all, not a fanatic. He merely insists on the overwhelming importance of justice or of purity of heart or of conscientiousness. He is offering us what can be a marvelously clarifying device for our moral vision. To keep insisting that other considerations also count can be like refusing to have our near-sightedness or our astigmatism corrected.

What begins to seem crucial to understanding the role of theories that offer at-top or at-bottom justifications of moral claims and to understanding their intolerance of competing moral truisms to those that are enshrined as central to the theory is the role that theory plays vis-à-vis moral leadership. Have we misunderstood that role by thinking of it as timeless, analytic, transcultural—whereas it is better understood as the handmaiden of moral leadership? Is it what brings order, system, and rational defense to what is, in the first instance or in its primary role, a moral movement and awakening to a "new" moral world?

But if the task set for theory as the handmaiden of leadership were to show the primary importance of a truism that had before seemed but one of many and had in fact been largely overlooked, how can that task be accomplished? For if the thesis of this chapter is an acceptable one, there is a list of moral considerations, the items of which cannot be reduced to one another as subcases under or disguises for what is "really fundamental." But the theoretical enterprise seems to have just that as an objective: to reduce all considerations to one sort.

My suggestion is that moral language has this characteristic: it is so framed as to leave room for clarification or transcendence by the presentation of one truism as the prism through which we can see others. We can, by altering prisms, get new perspectives on the common life. Now, justice will be seen as transcendent; now, kindness; now, loyalty. Moral language is in this sense overdetermined with respect to the possibilities of moral justification. In offering a moral rationale for a line of action, we have at our disposal more than one sort of consideration. At the same time we have open to us the possibility of vastly emphasizing one over all of the others. To do so is not, so far, to be a moral fanatic, if by a fanatic we mean a person who is willing to ignore moral considerations in the interest of some overwhelming purpose. Moral considerations need not be ignored by a moral leader, but they may not be accorded their due either. That is the danger. To lay great weight on one sort of consideration may be to mislead those whose interest is simply in a morally defensible life and in morally justifiable action. It may mislead by providing a prism through which what is relevant may seem dim or distorted.

The demand that there should be one underlying moral truism is itself a moral move. It is to say that moral advance requires that this truism should be revealed as the criterion by which we are to assess other apparent truisms. To show this is rationally to consecrate a moral insight. It is, then, in the tension between the attempted rational consecration of particular moral perspectives and the need to keep before us the possibilities of other moral truisms for providing perspective that ethical theory takes the shape that it does—the shape of one-principle salients against inevitable counter examples.

So far I have argued that there are reasons for questioning a common conception of normative ethics, that its business is the defense of some theory that will have sole claim to efficacy in moral problem resolving and, consequently, in the justification of moral conclusions. I have suggested that the claims of standard theories are overblown, that the field of moral thought and action is a wider and richer one than the theories allow, and that they are, thus, reductive by nature.

In the effort to demonstrate the resistance of morality to reductive theoretical moves, I have offered lists of adjectives (and corresponding considerations), such as 'cruel', 'honest', 'just', and 'loyal', that defy easy classification under the canonical theories. It is time now to look more closely at the approaches to ethics that are suggested by this wider, richer, and more-difficult-to-classify field—a field traditionally called 'virtue ethics'. There can be virtues of acts and of institutions, but we will be primarily concerned with the virtues of persons. The first order of business, then, is to make as clear to ourselves as we can what kind of personal qualities the virtues are. To that enquiry we now turn.

PART 2

Toward a Nonreductive Virtue Ethics

Why, Sir, if the fellow does not think as he speaks, he is
lying; and I see not what honor he can propose to himself
from having the character of a lyar. But if he does really
think that there is no distinction between virtue and vice,
why, Sir, when he leaves our houses, let us count our
spoons.

—James Boswell, *The Life of Samuel Johnson*

If he was not always sufficiently instructed in his subject,
his knowledge was, at least, greater than could have been
attained by others in the same state. If his works were
sometimes unfinished, accuracy cannot reasonably be
expected from a man oppressed with want, which he has
no hope of relieving but by a speedy publication. The
insolence and resentment of which he is accused were not
easily to be avoided by a great mind irritated by perpetual
hardships, and constrained hourly to return the spurns of
contempt, and repress the insolence of prosperity. . . .
Those are no proper judges of his conduct who have
slumbered away their time on the down of plenty; nor
will any wise man say, "Had I been in Savage's condition,
I should have lived or written better than Savage."

—Samuel Johnson, *Lives of the Poets*

5

Two Cheers for Meno:
The Definition of the Virtues

Socrates: What do you yourself say virtue is?

Meno: First of all, if it is manly virtue you are after, it is easy to see that the virtue of a man consists in managing the city's affairs capably, and so that he will help his friends and injure his foes while taking care to come to no harm himself. Or if you want a woman's virtue, that is easily described. She must be a good housewife, careful with her stores and obedient to her husband. Then there is another virtue for a child, male or female, and another for an old man, free or slave as you like; and a great many more kinds of virtue.

Socrates: I seem to be in luck. I wanted one virtue and I find that you have a whole swarm of virtues to offer.

—Plato, *Meno*

Meno must surely rank as one of the easiest to push over of Socratic respondents; but if he had just pursued it, he could have salvaged two or three points from his weak beginning. One point, overlooked by nearly every contemporary philosopher who attempts a definition, is that if we are to understand what virtue is, it might be well to begin

"Two Cheers for Meno" was partially incorporated in "Virtue, the Quality of Life, and Punishment," in *Monist* 63, no. 2 (Apr. 1980). It was reprinted, with additions, in *Virtue and Medicine*, ed. Earl Shelp (D. Reidel, 1985). I should like to thank my (then) University of Texas colleagues for their criticisms of an earlier version of this chapter—particularly Robert Audi, Thomas Seung, and Douglas Browning.

with a list of qualities that we intuitively recognize as virtues and vices. A second point is that it may, for some qualities, depend on the context (city or household, for example) whether they are virtues or vices or neither. A third point is that by distinguishing different sorts of virtue, we will be in a better position to evaluate answers to such large questions as whether virtue can be taught, whether virtue is one, and whether virtue is knowledge. In this chapter, I will offer a preliminary survey that could be useful in arriving at nuanced answers to these large questions.

Meno gets off to a bad start, not because he tries to distinguish sorts of virtue, but because he begins with an inadequate sorting scheme. Socrates maintains that justice is justice, whether predicated of a man or a woman, and that to speak meaningfully of justice in the city or in the household, we must have a notion of what justice is wherever it is exhibited. So the range to be covered by an adequate definition of virtue is indicated by terms such as 'justice' and 'temperance', rather then by such terms as 'female virtue' and 'male virtue', 'slave virtue' and 'freeman's virtue'. But if this is the range and if we can add an indefinitely long list of terms that intuitively belong within it, then why should we suppose that there is a yes or a no answer to such questions as whether virtue can be taught? Far from presupposing that there is one answer to such questions, we might even use them as means of differentiating sorts of virtue: virtues that can and cannot be taught, virtues that do and do not consist in or require knowing something, and so forth.

But if Meno rates two cheers, Socrates rates two and one-half, for Socrates recognizes the difficulty of defining the virtues, as Meno does not. Socrates arrives at no definition; he arrives only at a hypothesis concerning the origin of virtue, which is irrelevant, as he recognizes, to the question of what virtue is. This negative conclusion—that no satisfactory definition of virtue has been found—is the note on which the *Meno* ends; but Socratic modesty is not a characteristic of recent writing on the concept of virtue. At the end of this chapter, I will mention some contemporary definitions of virtue that have, I believe, been too confidently put forward.

Well short of definition, some preliminary things can and need to be said about where virtues and vices belong. They are qualities of persons; and the first problem is to set them off from other sorts of qualities that persons may have. Some qualities or properties may be of persons but not be personal qualities. For example, being attracted by gravity is a property of every person (with the possible exception of angels), but we would not want to call that property a personal one. It does not enable us to distinguish between persons; and that is what I will take as a necessary characteristic of a personal property. On the other hand, some qualities that do enable us to distinguish between persons do not yet seem to be personal in the appropriate sense, the sense in which they are relevant to the kind of distinction that we would like to make. Thus, some persons maintain a body temperature of 98.1° Fahrenheit, whereas others maintain a temperature of 97.9°; some have black hair, and some have red. That Rocky has red hair tells us something about him as a person only if we associate having red hair with properties of a different sort, such as being pugnacious or aggressive.

As a first approximation, we can say that virtues and vices are a subclass of those properties referred to in answer to the question "What kind of person is Wiggins?" Not all answers to that question consist of a list of properties. One sort of answer is to tell a revealing story; another is to smile approvingly or to frown and shake one's head. It is also clear that not just any list of properties, such as "born in Chicago" or "over 150 pounds," will do. Another sort of answer, closer to the mark, will not do either. It does not tell us, except by inference from the speaker's values, what sort of person Wiggins is if the speaker replies that he is good, bad, odd, praiseworthy, wonderful, or despicable. To understand these remarks, we must find our what sort of person the speaker would count as good, and so forth. He has not told us so much what kind of person Wiggins is as what the speaker's opinion of him is. The terms that the speaker uses are descriptively empty; whereas we want description, or at least some descriptive content, but descriptive content of a certain sort. A third kind of answer won't do either. We can't say what kind of person Wiggins is by mentioning merely transient or ephemeral qualities. It won't do to say that he is bored or that he is angry, unless what is meant is that he is typically a bored person or an 'angry man'.

As a second move, let's spread before us the names of some qualities that can serve as answers to the question as to what kind of person Wiggins is. Here is a list of such names.*

able	cooperative	friendly	magnanimous
affable	cosmopolitan	frugal	manly
affected	courageous	gallant	mannerly
affectionate	courteous	gay	meek
agreeable	courtly	generous	mercenary
alacritous	covetous	gentle	mercurial
ambitious	credulous	good-living	methodical
amiable	cruel	good-natured	moderate
argumentative	curious	good-tempered	modest
arrogant	dastardly	grouchy	morbid
avaricious	decent	hasty	nefarious
belligerent	dedicated	helpful	neurotic
benevolent	dependable	honest	odd
bilious	devout	hospitable	open-minded
boastful	dictatorial	humble	opinionated
brainy	dignified	humorous	orderly
brave	disciplined	idle	patronizing
brooding	disgraceful	imperturbable	peevish
bullying	distant	impulsive	persistent
calculating	distinguished	independent	pessimistic
callous	dominating	inflexible	petulant
cantankerous	domineering	ingenious	phlegmatic
careful	ebullient	ingenuous	picayune
cautious	energetic	inscrutable	polite
changeable	enigmatic	intelligent	pompous
charitable	enterprising	interesting	prescient
cheerful	envious	irritable	presumptuous
civil	equable	jingoistic	pretentious
claustrophobic	euphemistic	jocular	proud
clever	excitable	jovial	prudent
cold	exhibitionistic	just	quarrelsome
complacent	fair-minded	kindly	queer
complaisant	fearful	knightly	querulous
conceited	flattering	lazy	quick-witted
condescending	foolish	learned	quizzical
conscienceless	foresighted	light-hearted	reasonable
conscientious	forgiving	lively	refined
contrary	frank	lustful	reliable

* This list was compiled jointly with Robert Audi.

religious	serious	tender-minded	virile
repressed	shy	tense	vivacious
reserved	silly	thoughtful	waspish
respectable	simple	thoughtless	watchful
respectful	simple-minded	threatening	weak
revengeful	sensible	thrifty	weak-minded
secretive	sinful	timid	well-intentioned
self-confident	slavish	tolerant	whimsical
self-contained	sober	torpid	wise
self-controlled	spoiled	truthful	withdrawn
self-disciplined	stimulating	uncomplaining	witty
self-indulgent	stubborn	undemonstra-	worrying
selfish	stupid	tive	xenophobic
self-pitying	submissive	understanding	yielding
self-reliant	suggestible	uxorious	youthful
self-respecting	sympathetic	vigorous	zany
self-satisfied	tactful	vindictive	zealous
sensitive	tender		

These properties do have some common features. They are not static ones, such as specifying weight or place or birth; they are dynamic, having to do with tendencies, or dispositions. They concern the way in which Wiggins typically moves through life—his reactions and attitudes, as well as his actions. They also seem, at least potentially, to be grounds for preference or avoidance. But the preference or avoidance is of a different sort from that in which we would, for example, prefer a person who weighs over 150 pounds for an experiment in nutrition or would avoid a person raised in Chicago if we wanted a good example of a Southern accent. Furthermore, although these properties are (for short) dispositional, the dispositions in question are determinable, as opposed to determinate ones. A disposition to blush upon hearing a certain word, to tremble, to mispronounce 'nuclear', or to blink rapidly is determinate. The term for the disposition is descriptive, in a straightforward physical way, of just what the person does. We could teach a child what 'tremble' or 'blink rapidly' mean by showing him people who tremble and who blink rapidly. We could construct dolls for him that act and react in these determinate ways, but it is open to conceptual question whether ingenious technicians could construct dolls for him that would act and react in the ways appropriate to the properties on our list. These properties are determinable. You cannot teach a child what charitability is by showing him someone putting money in the hands of another person. There are indefinitely many ways, not just one way, in which charitability can be evinced. The terms on our list vary in their determinability, but none of them is determined in the sense just indicated.

S ome sorts of persons we prefer; others we avoid. The properties on our list can serve as reasons for preference or for avoidance. If we are asked to pick out both the virtues on our list and the vices, then, I suggest, we will be looking for dispositional grounds for preference or avoidance. We might think that cruel people are nearly always to be avoided and that cheerful ones are nearly always to be preferred; but we may think that it depends much more heavily on the circumstances whether ambitious persons are to be preferred or complacent ones are to be avoided. I suggest that the natural home of the language of virtue and vice is in that region of our lives in which we must choose between, not acts, lines of action, or policies, but persons. Persons, unlike acts or policies, are not right or wrong, beneficent or disastrous, although policies or acts, like persons, can be cruel or just. I will not take up here the question of the relations between the virtues of persons and of acts, policies, or practices.

'Choosing between persons' is, of course, a very global sort of expression. Sometimes we must, quite directly, choose A or B or C, where all are candidates for the same job, public office, or scholarship. Sometimes we must choose, not between persons, but whether, and with what reservations, to enter into some relationship with a particular person, such as a landlord, tenant, lawyer, contractor, wife, friend, confidant, or guest. These choices, once made, can lead to further and yet further choices, at many levels and of many degrees. We must not only choose relationships; we must continually adjust to them in a variety of ways, depending upon our assessment of other people and of ourselves. We can think of the language of virtue as providing the set of categories in terms of which we can justify our choices of persons.

Suppose no choice could be made between persons. This could be so if it were impossible to distinguish between 'persons', or if the 'choice' were made for us. If we lived in a world of identical creatures, then the determination of who should be president and who should be hod carrier would be an arbitrary one; or if the 'choice' were made *for* us between nonidenticals, we would have no occasion for the justification of choice, for the adducement of grounds.

I am not sure whether any philosophers would deny that virtues and vices are dispositional properties that provide grounds for preference or for avoidance of persons. There are at least three possible objections to a dispositional analysis. The first might arise on the part of a reader who has been accustomed to thinking of character traits as matters of habit, rather than of disposition. So he will not be ready to concede the laurels to disposition as a matter of definition. The crux of the matter seems to be that to say of a person that he has a habit of doing anything is to imply that at some time or other, he learned to do it and that he might have learned otherwise, that it would have been possible for him to do so had he so chosen. It always makes sense, given that Wiggins has a habit of doing something, to ask when he learned (or picked up or acquired) the habit. The implication, correctly or incorrectly, is that if he learned it, he might have learned some other habit instead, so that he is *responsible* for what he does as a result of the habit. It is not an excuse, to put the matter another way, that what Wiggins did was a result of habit, since if what he did was wrong, Wiggins should not have such habits. To begin by making personality traits, and hence character traits, dispositions is, so the objection might go, to settle the fundamental question of responsibility by definitional fiat.

Two answers can be given in justification of a preference for 'dispositions' over 'habits'. The first is that 'habit' is a term of very narrow scope. There are a great many traits that are clearly neither habits nor the result of a habit. It would be stretching the term unmercifully to refer to cleverness, stupidity, or cupidity as habits. There would be no answers to the questions as to when we acquired the habits in question, what we had done to encourage them, or whether we might not now break them. Not only this; there are a great many habits that are evidence for dispositions. For example, the habit of twitching one's foot is evidence for the proposition that a person is nervous. The second answer is that speaking of dispositions allows us to capture more easily the language by which we assess character. Dispositions are determinables; habits are typically determinate. When we say that Wiggins has a habit of tipping his hat to ladies, we say exactly what he does in certain circumstances; but when we say that he is polite, we do not. Courage is not just the habit of leading, instead of following, one's troops; it involves other habits as well. In fact, to the extent that action can be shown to be 'merely' habitual, then Wiggins's doing that thing is not evidence of his courage.

I suspect that the preference for habit over disposition arises partly through confusion. The inculcation of habits may be the best way to develop dispositions. That is why we can give children 'moral training'. But moral training, at best, is imparting habits that are likely to bring about appropriate dispositions. Otto can quite easily be taught the habit of tipping his hat; but it does not follow that he can easily be taught to be polite, unless by politeness is meant merely the habitual performance of such rituals. No less a question than whether virtue can be taught is at issue here; but to speak of personality traits and, hence, of character traits as habits would offer us an all-too-facile answer. Of course, habits can be taught; but we cannot resolve so difficult a problem by so simple a move.

The second source of discomfort with a definition of personality traits as dispositions may arise from a behavioral interpretation of 'disposition', as in the paradigmatic dispositional term 'brittle'. A kind of material is brittle if when struck it shatters; similarly, 'disposition' may be thought to refer always to publicly observable behavior. But the objector rightly wants to reserve a place for the 'inner' dispositions or tendencies to feel, to experience emotion, to sense the feelings of others, to react privately. These, too, must be taken into account in the assessment of character; and if by definition they are excluded, then the definition must be refashioned. The answer to this objection is simply that I agree and that it is not my intention to define disposition behaviorally. Dispositions, as I understand the term, are not just tendencies to act in certain ways but also to feel, to think, and to react and to experience 'passions'. I do not need to take a position on the confused question of whether these feelings and the like can somehow be 'reduced' to external behavior. Whether or not they can, I wish to include them in the data on which we should rely in the attribution of traits of personality, and hence of character traits.

Finally, it might be objected that, leaving aside the question of 'internal' versus 'external' dispositions, it is a mistake to define personality or character traits in terms of dispositions at all, since a person's character can be established by one incident in his lifetime. For example, the objector might continue, no matter what else he might have done in his lifetime, Ivan Karamasov's nobleman was a cruel man because he set his hunting pack upon a serf child who had injured the paw of the nobleman's hunting dog. Nothing that the nobleman could do afterwards would make this an unjust or unwarranted accusation. The one incident alone is enough to establish his character. But the objector must answer the question of why he feels there is nothing that Karamasov's nobleman can do to erase the cruelty of his character. I suggest that it is because the objector feels that the nobleman's carefully planned nonaccidental deed *reveals* his character in a way that less dramatically cruel deeds might not. The objector believes that a man who could do such a thing could not be otherwise than cruel. The man's nature has been exhibited, and it cannot henceforth be successfully concealed. But what is the objector saying if not that the deed reveals a covert disposition? I would not wish to deny that there are dispositions that can be more or less successfully concealed. It is undeniable that men do sometimes reveal themselves by a single dramatic action and that unless he was insane or otherwise ineligible for judgment, our nobleman *was* indeed a cruel man. This is a place to pay attention to tenses. I would be most hesitant to say that henceforward, throughout his lifetime, he *is* a cruel man. That would be to take the dubious moral and psychological stand that no transformation of character is possible for a person who has descended to such depths of cruelty. I am not at all sure that this is true. I do not say that he should not be ashamed of his action for the rest of his life or that he has not done something inexcusably wrong. I do not want to argue that the transformation of character somehow releases a person from the opprobrium that he has rightly incurred for his past action. In any case, the objection presupposes a dispositional interpretation of personality traits, because the one deed supposedly reveals a covert disposition. Since I am willing to grant that dispositions may sometimes be success-fully concealed, there is no argument.

If we understand virtues and vices as dispositional proper-ties that provide grounds for preference or avoidance of persons, then the list will be indefinitely long, and it will be functionally various. There can be *many* different sorts of reason for preference, some of which we will survey in a moment; and a definition of virtue that picks out one or a very few dispositions as constituting the whole of virtue must shoulder the burden of showing that it is not unjustifia-bly reductive. Thus, for Kant, conscientiousness is *the* virtue; for Mill, *the* virtue is benevolence; for some ancient philoso-phers, there were four cardinal virtues; and the church fathers, accepting these, were willing to add only three theological ones. Yet unless there is some prior reason to believe that there is but one or that there are but very few bases for preference of persons, the reductive mode of analysis may be misconceived from the beginning. Why should we suppose that only conscientiousness matters in preferring one person to another, or only benevolence, or only the cardinal virtues? A dozen neglected dispositions come to mind. What reason do we have to suppose that they can all be neatly tucked under the favored qualities? Why should we say of a person who is careful, cautious, charita-ble, cheerful, clever, civil, cooperative, and courteous that the only reason for preferring him to others is, really, that he is conscientious or that he is just? To say this is to imply that either these other apparent grounds for preference and choice are not such or that the dispositions in question are really the favored dispositions in disguise or that they are derivable in some way from them. But that would then remain to be shown; and I do not know of any place where it is shown.

A more promising way of encompassing virtue than nominating some one or a few virtues as the only real ones is to look more carefully at preference and choice of persons, to ask of the philosopher who would restrict the virtues so radically what sort of choice he has in mind. What are the most general grounds of choice that must be made of persons? That is not a small question; but it would seem that until we have attained some clarity on it, we will be unable to show what dispositions provide grounds for choice. This might make it seem as if we should start again with Meno and say that there is one set of grounds for choosing or preferring slaves, another for freemen; one set for men and another for women; and so on. In slaves we will want obedience, patience, and vigorousness, say. But since there are as many categories of persons as there are bees, such an approach will yield an unordered 'swarm of virtues'. For there are old and young slaves, field slaves and house slaves, and on and on. But if my suggestion is correct, virtue and vice terms are best understood as answers to the question of what sort of person Wiggins is, not just what sort of slave, freeman, athlete, poet, and so forth, he is. (Of course we can speak, not of virtue proper, but of the virtues of slaves, and so on. This is not what Socrates wanted, and it is not what is wanted for moral philosophy.) If I am correct—if V is a virtue—then to say that A is V is to provide a reason why A should be preferred to other persons, whatever A's status, even though for a particular status one sort of virtue may be more relevant to choice than another. The first task, then, is to survey the most general grounds for preference of persons. Such a survey is, I think, the best antidote to reductive definitions. A beginning sketch of such a survey is presented in the chart on page 85.

A way of beginning to distinguish the grounds of preference for or choice of persons and, hence, of categorizing the virtues (for simplicity I ignore the vices) is to set off considerations that have to do with the aptness or appropriateness of the person for the accomplishment or achievement of goals or objectives, from considerations that do not have to do with these teleological intentions (cf. chart, p. 85). Let me begin, then, by speaking of *instrumental* versus *noninstrumental* virtues. Instrumental virtues in a person are those that, in relatively direct fashion, make it more probable that he will successfully pursue goals, ends, or objectives.

If we were to pursue this distinction in more detail, it would be necessary, with a bow to Ryle, to distinguish these qualities from another set with which they might be confused: the virtues that concern the doing of tasks well, as opposed to the present set—those that concern pursuing goals successfully. There are task virtues such as neatness, thoroughness, carefulness, and sensitivity that fall in the first class; virtues such as persistence, alertness, and courage fall more naturally in the second, the instrumental, class. The instrumental virtues are at home in talk about winning wars, finding the sources of rivers, finishing novels, reducing deficits, and crossing oceans. The task virtues are at home in talk about bricklaying, painting, gardening, and typing, where we can and do distinguish the question of how successful the overall undertaking was from the question of how well it was done. A good bricklayer may be either a person who gets the job done quickly (and passably well) or one who is unusually neat or artistic.

The easiest and most obvious side of this overall classification is the instrumental one. Persons, as individuals, are more likely to succeed in undertakings of any difficulty if they are persistent enough not to be easily discouraged, courageous enough to face daunting challenges, alert enough to perceive pitfalls and opportunities, careful enough not to make needless errors, resourceful enough to devise alternative strategies, prudent enough to plan ahead for eventualities that are likely to be encountered, energetic and strong enough to carry through what they have planned, cool-headed enough to meet emergencies without panicking, and confident and determined enough not to give way to evanescent feelings and desires that would lead them away from their tasks. In addition, there are qualities that make persons worthy of preference for participation in joint or communal undertakings, such as cooperativeness, the virtues of leaders and followers, and the kind of practical

Personality Traits

VIRTUES

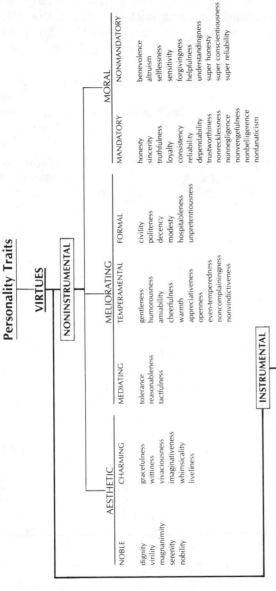

NONINSTRUMENTAL

AESTHETIC

NOBLE

dignity
virility
magnanimity
serenity
nobility

CHARMING

gracefulness
wittiness
vivaciousness
imaginativeness
whimsicality
liveliness

MELIORATING

MEDIATING

tolerance
reasonableness
tactfulness

TEMPERAMENTAL

gentleness
humorousness
amiability
cheerfulness
warmth
appreciativeness
openness
even-temperedness
noncomplainingness
nonvindictiveness

FORMAL

civility
politeness
decency
modesty
hospitableness
unpretentiousness

MORAL

MANDATORY

honesty
sincerity
truthfulness
loyalty
consistency
reliability
dependability
trustworthiness
nonrecklessness
nonnegligence
nonvengefulness
nonbelligerence
nonfanaticism

NONMANDATORY

benevolence
altruism
selflessness
sensitivity
forgivingness
helpfulness
understandingness
super honesty
super conscientiousness
super reliability

INSTRUMENTAL

AGENT INSTRUMENTAL

persistence
courage
alertness
carefulness
resourcefulness
prudence
energy
strength
cool-headedness
determination

GROUP INSTRUMENTAL

cooperativeness
'practical wisdom'
the virtues of leaders
and followers

wisdom about the best means to ends that comes from experience in group endeavors, the sort of wisdom that has to do with the division and apportionment of tasks and the choice of appropriate social structures and instruments for the undertaking at hand.

The noninstrumental virtues are a more varied lot; they are a good deal more intriguing candidates for analysis. They may make the attainment of individual or group goals more or less likely, but if so, their contribution is not a direct one, and they are not typically valued for that reason. Some noninstrumental virtues have no easily detectable relation to success in individual or joint undertakings. I will speak of three general sorts of noninstrumental virtues: aesthetic, meliorating, and moral.

Aesthetic virtues are qualities that are farthest away from being instrumentally valued or depreciated. Aesthetic virtues are appreciated for what they are, for the vision of themselves; we are grateful for their presence; they are exemplars of what humans can be; their absence is regretted because it impoverishes life. There are at least two general sorts of aesthetic virtues: the noble and the charming. Noble virtues include dignity, virility, magnanimity, serenity, and, of course, nobility itself. The similarity to the Stoic list of virtues is not accidental. The Stoic's objectives seem to have been twofold: to achieve serenity—a certain level or tone in life—and to make of oneself a kind of model of what humans might aspire to, a model of nobility, of the sort of person who lives and dies in a high and admirable way.

Charming virtues attract, not by their altitude, but by their beauty. We appreciate gracefulness in a person: gracefulness in posture, in movement, in expression, in meeting the ordinary exigencies of life. Wittiness can be charming, as can liveliness, imaginativeness, and whimsicality. People who have such qualities attract, simply because life is better with such people than without them. The corresponding vices make for dull and unattractive common life: ungracefulness, lack of wit, and so on.

Meliorating virtues occupy a middle range on the instrumental/noninstrumental continuum. I have placed them on the noninstrumental side because their contribution to common life is not the direct one of making success in individual or common endeavor more likely; it is, rather, the making of common life, whether or not it is structured for common endeavor, more tolerable. This dark description may perhaps be brightened by the sorts of examples I will give. In general, there seem to me to be at least three sorts of meliorating virtues: mediating, temperamental, and formal.

Given that in the ordinary course of life, differences, disputes, and quarrels are likely to arise, peacemakers, negotiators, and appeasers are needed; and the qualities appropriate to these roles are generally valued: tolerance of views and attitudes that are different from one's own, reasonableness in assessing opposing points of view, and tactfulness in not arousing unnecessary hostilities. These, then, are *mediating* virtues; they will be more or less emphasized as the historical, sociological, and particular and personal circumstances demand; but it is hard to conceive of a human situation in which they will not have value.

Like other meliorating virtues, the mediating virtues have value in a less-than-perfect world. In a world, like the Distant Earth in Dostoyevsky's *Dream of a Ridiculous Man*, in which everyone truly loved one another and there were never ever invidious comparisons, frictions, or disputes, there would be no place for mediating virtues; and the next sorts of qualities I want to discuss, the temperamental and formal ones, would be simply taken for granted as to be expected in everyone and, hence, would not count as virtues at all.

Temperamental virtues form a large class. Their general characteristic is simply that the persons who have them are easier and more pleasant to live with, that the avoidance of the corresponding vices constitutes a gain in communal life. Let me mention a few: gentleness, humorousness, amiability, cheerfulness, warmth, appreciativeness, openness, even-temperedness, noncomplainingness, and nonvindictiveness. The most direct road to appreciation of the temperamental virtues is to focus on the corresponding vices, to think what life is like in the presence of vindictiveness, continual complaints, frequent outbursts of temper, and so on.

There is a special problem about the temperamental virtues signaled by the label that I have given to them. If they are matters of temperament, then how can they be virtues at all? If virtues are qualities for which the bearer is to some degree responsible and if different people, like different breeds of horses or dogs, may just be the happy or unhappy possessors of a particular temperament, given by birth, how can there be temperamental virtues? I have not, however, wanted to confine the field of virtue and vice to qualities for which the agent is responsible. It is, I think, merely a philosophical superstition that virtue need be so confined. We can and do prefer and avoid people on account of qualities they have when we have not the least idea whether they may justly be held responsible for these qualities. Some people may well inherit qualities or acquire them so early that they cannot be said to have any control over their acquisition, and these qualities may nonetheless provide substantial grounds for preference or avoidance. Preference and avoidance must not be thought of as instruments for moral training by means of which we induce people to develop certain qualities. Sometimes, even often, we may prefer or avoid a person for qualities that we do not praise or blame him for having.

This is not to say that there are no degrees of responsibility for what I have labeled 'temperamental virtues'. Some of them may be, to some extent, under the control of the agent. If he tries to change himself, he can be more cheerful or open. Perhaps the least tractable of the virtues that I have mentioned is humorousness. If a person has no sense of humor, then he can hardly be blamed for being humorless. One can't give oneself a sense of humor in the way that one can, to some extent, give oneself cheerfulness. A sense of humor depends on a certain capacity to catch the point of a joke or to see the funny side of things; cheerfulness can be forced, and if forced enough and in the right way, it can become second nature. But even if a person cannot be blamed for humorlessness, we would prefer the person with a sense of humor to the one without it; and we will always have a residual suspicion that if it is (to use the language of Samuel Butler) not a person's fault that he has no sense of humor, it is nevertheless a fault in him. He is too narrowly focused on the literal and the everyday, too little concerned with side perspectives, with the leavening of the flat and the ordinary. Humorlessness may in fact be symptomatic of a whole syndrome of qualities, some of which *are* changeable by the agent's efforts.

However that may be, there is a third group of meliorating virtues that we must now notice: the *formal* virtues. These include civility, politeness, decency, and hospitableness. Their common characteristic is that they meliorate by adhering to customs, common understandings, or practices that themselves meliorate. The practices that fall under the general heading of courtesy simply make common life more liveable, easier, more pleasant, and less strained by confrontation and by push and shove. It is not easy or pleasant to live with persons who are incivil and impolite, have no decency, or are habitually inhospitable.

There is a particular sort of noninstrumental virtue that deserves separate treatment. Persons who exhibit the virtues and vices in question are regarded in a special sort of way—a way that can be distinguished from the way in which those persons are held whose virtues and vices are aesthetically pleasing or displeasing or are generally meliorating or exacerbating. These virtues and vices have the common characteristic that they are forms of regard or lack of regard for the interests of others. They are, roughly, of two closely related classes: those that have to do with direct concern or lack of concern for the interests of other persons, on the one hand, and those that have to do with the unfair advantage that one accords to one's own interests over the interests of others.

While the meliorating virtues and, of course, the instrumental ones are *in* the interests of others, the unifying characteristic of the present lot of virtues is that they are traits concerned with the regard that *the agent has* for the interests of others. What makes them virtues or vices is, essentially, the agent's acting or his failing to act out of a certain sort of motive; but there is no motive that provides a distinguishing characteristic of meliorating virtues.

What many people must have in mind when they speak of the demands of morality and when they deplore the absence of 'moral' qualities in others (and in themselves) is that people take unfair advantage in their own interest or in the interest of those with whom they identify. Most of what are regarded as moral qualities can, I think, be seen to involve some form of this failing or sin. Various forms of nondeceptiveness—for example, honesty, sincerity, truthfulness—fall under the general requirement that no unfair advantage be taken. It is always in the power of the person who is conveying information to edit or distort it to his own advantage, if advantage is to be gained by misleading the hearer; the person being trusted can always violate the trust to his own advantage; the insincere person can profess what he does not believe or hold, thereby hoping to gain an advantage to which he is not entitled. The unfairness in these cases consists in this: that the dishonest, insincere, or untruthful person does what any other *could* do in his own interest but what others generally refrain from doing to their own occasional loss. It is unprincipled opportunism that is unfair, if others, who have as much to gain, are governed by principle. This quality is peculiarly evil in a system that depends on mutual trust and on self-government, rather than on coercion. This is one way of thinking of a moral community. Moral communities are notoriously fragile structures, and the unprincipled opportunist takes advantage of their existence while at the same time undermining them.[1]

There are other ways, in addition to deceptiveness, of taking unfair advantage of others. One can be disloyal, for example, where another person has a right to expect loyalty. One can be inconstant, in that one does not faithfully adhere to the principles that one has led others to believe that one holds. One can be unreliable, undependable, untrustworthy—giving assurances or accepting responsibilities that one does not then live up to. One can be reckless, taking chances with other people's lives in a careening vehicle; one can be negligent, not taking the precautions that may rightly be expected of one. One can be cruel or vengeful, 'acting out', at others' expense—and as others could do but do not—the frustrations or vindictiveness that one feels. One can be belligerent against a general background of civility, thereby gaining one's way. One can be fanatical in the pursuit of one's objectives, thus placing those objectives above the interests of everyone else. These are all ways of taking unfair advantage of those who are, by and large, self-disciplined, nondeceptive, loyal, conscientious, constant, and so on.

The moral community is the community of persons who, generally, are self-governed and conscientious, and it cannot long contain persons who are not. Because there are no external sanctions, such as imprisonment or transportation, that correspond to moral failings, the moral community can preserve itself only by shame, blame, and excommunication. If shame and blame have no leverage on an individual and if he continues, in the many ways possible, to take unfair advantage, then he must somehow be labeled; people must be warned that he is not, though he pretends to be, a member of the community, that he has no conscience, that he is not to be trusted, that he is a fanatic. But if he is not a member of the moral community, there will be few circumstances in which he will be chosen or preferred; it is in this sense that the 'moral' virtues and vices are especially fundamental ones. We can think of circumstances in which it is not especially important that a person be persistent, courageous, graceful, or gentle; but we can think of few if any circumstances in which deceptiveness or unreliability are not important. Although it is true that fanaticism in some narrow cause or that disloyalty to particular persons might not matter in some choices between and of persons, we would in nearly any circumstance beware of the person who is 'loyal to no one but himself' or whose life obviously revolves closely around his fanatical cause.

There are persons who, far from taking unfair advantage of others, are especially concerned to take the interests of others into account. There are kind, benevolent, altruistic, generous, charitable, selfless, forgiving, sensitive, helpful, and understanding people. While the absence of these qualities is not necessarily a vice, their presence is a virtue, a reason why such persons are to be preferred to persons who do not have those qualities. These are the nonmandatory 'moral' virtues. It is possible to be overly selfless, altruistic, benevolent, and so forth. The person who entirely forgets and has no regard for his own interest is not necessarily worthy of respect. Saint Francis of Assisi is a moral model of limited relevance; it is hard to reconcile true selflessness with self-respect and dignity, which are also qualities that provide reasons for preference, or with the instrumental qualities that depend for their motivating force on the vividness and interest of personal goals.

Some, but not all, of the mandatory moral virtues have nonmandatory counterparts. One can be honest or loyal beyond the requirements of duty. Other moral virtues have no such counterparts: nonfanaticism and nonnegligence, for example. Here, to have a virtue is simply not to have a vice. But as with honesty, there are a number of mandatory moral virtues that can be oversubscribed; persons are blameworthy if they do not come up to the minimum; they are praiseworthy to the extent that they exceed it. A person can be superbly or marvelously conscientious and reliable, well beyond the requirements of the demand that he not take unfair advantage of others by being unconcerned about his duty or about fulfilling his commitments.

Justice is, on the present analysis and in agreement with well-known predecessors, the quintessentially moral virtue—if justice is understood broadly to include not making a special case of oneself, not making exceptions where others make none, or not taking advantage of one's own position. One cannot, thus, oversubscribe justice. There is another sense of justice, once-removed from the above and more narrowly applicable: the justice that is a virtue of those persons—such as judges, administrators, employers, teachers—who make distributions between persons of what is wanted or disliked. Here the issue is not, ideally, the directly moral one of taking unfair advantage in one's own interest but of seeing to it that there is no unfair advantage given to other persons, the recipients of the distribution. The distributor of jobs, punishments, funds, housing, grades, or whatever, has as a part of his business to see that like cases are treated alike and that different cases are treated differently. Again, one cannot be *too* just. But it does not follow that justice is the only virtue, that it is 'the central' one, or even that there is a 'central' virtue.

A useful way of defining the 'cardinal' virtues would be as those virtues of which there cannot be too much. This would rule out persistence and some other instrumental virtues, cheerfulness and some other meliorating virtues; it would leave, among others, the central moral virtue of justice. To say that there cannot be too much of a virtue is to imply that having a lot of that virtue does not take away from having other virtues that one considers important. The cardinal virtues must be compatible in this sense. Plato thought that you couldn't have too much of any cardinal virtue because, virtue being one, being very courageous can't conflict with being very just; Aristotle thought that you couldn't have too much of any virtue because he thought of all virtues as means between extremes. But on the very wide definition of virtues as qualities that (ordinarily) give grounds for preference, one *can* have too much of some virtues.

While it is not the primary purpose of this chapter to set out a distinction between moral virtues and vices as opposed to other virtues and vices, the present suggestion does seem attractive, and before leaving it, I want to mention a few of its advantages.

The first, the most obvious, is that it provides a way of accounting for the peculiar importance attached to the moral virtues. There are very many ways of taking unfair advantage of other persons; doing so constitutes an especially repugnant practice. It amounts to rejection of the other person, of using him, of denying consideration to him, or of regarding him as a mere obstacle, a hindrance to one's own interests.

The second advantage is just that by looking at the variety of moral virtues and vices, one is led to consider the subtle and various ways in which taking unfair advantage can become a part of personality. The differences between the different forms of deceptiveness, the proper demands of conscience, the requirements of loyalty—all of these are matters that can be underlined by the present distinction between moral and other virtues and vices.

A third advantage is the sharp line that is drawn between egoism and morality. Egoism is not a moral theory on a par with others, but it is precisely a theory to the effect that one should not be moral, since being moral requires one on occasion to sacrifice one's own interest. And the inevitable consequence of concern for the interest of others is precisely that one must sometimes sacrifice one's own interest.

Finally, conscientiousness is put in its place. What is morally important is not just acting from duty, however duty is construed, but also acting under rules or practices that are fair to all, in a way that is fair to others who are acting under those rules or practices.

In this chapter, I have tried to provide a generous-enough survey of the types of virtue to include most of the qualities that are or may be regarded as virtues or vices. I have viewed this as necessary if we are to avoid definitions or understandings of virtues that are in any way reductive. Some contemporary definitions, while appropriate or insightful in other ways, do seem to me to have this character. It is to these definitions that I now turn.

G. H. von Wright, in his otherwise acute discussion of virtue in *The Varieties of Goodness*, tells us that "the role of a virtue, to put it briefly, is to counteract, eliminate, rule out the obscuring effects which emotion may have on our own practical judgment, i.e., judgment relating to the beneficient or harmful nature of a chosen course of action."[2]

This definition has the classical defect of philosophical definitions: it is at once too narrow and too broad. It is too narrow in that it would not count as virtues those qualities that have little if anything to do with the overcoming of obscuring emotion. The person who is the happy possessor of the instrumental virtues of self-confidence and resourcefulness need not be overcoming any obscuring emotion in exhibiting them; the same may be said for the mediating virtues of open-mindedness and tactfulness, the aesthetic virtues of gracefulness and dignity, and the meliorating virtues of gentleness and cheerfulness. It is too broad in that if moral virtue is what is in question and to the extent that it is true of moral virtue that it consists in the ruling out of obscuring emotion, then it does not help us to identify the emotions in question or to say why overruling them is peculiarly important to morality. I am not sure whether to call the desire to take unfair advantage an emotion; but this desire is at least a morally important one. The emotions that need overruling, from the present point of view, are those that would prevent the agent from taking proper account of the interests of others and would thus lead him to give undue weight to his own interests.

Lester Hunt contends that "a person has a trait of character insofar as he holds the corresponding belief and holds it as a principle: insofar, that is, as he believe it, and acts on it consistently (for both of these things admit of degrees)."[3] To have traits of character, he tells us, is to have reasons for what one does, of the sort that brutes cannot have. But it is not clear what is to be gained by a definition that rules out such qualities as cheerfulness, imaginativeness, civility, gracefulness, and resourcefulness as qualities of character. For these qualities and very many others, it is difficult to see that any special belief need be held in order for the quality to be present. This is to say nothing about the problem of identifying the corresponding belief.

Hunt comes closer to the mark if his definition is interpreted as applying to moral character. Then, the belief in question might, as I have suggested, be that one should take the interests of others seriously and that one should not take unfair advantage. But the difficulty here is in giving an account of having a corresponding principle that does not beg the question of whether traits of moral character are necessarily accompanied by principles. Why a person cannot just be concerned for the interests of others and be fair, without holding a principle, is not clear.

Maurice Mandelbaum tells us that "the traditionally acknowledged virtues are . . . precisely those traits of character which provide fitting answers to the ever-recurring demands which all men face."[4] 'Character' refers to the "relatively persistent forms which a person's motivation takes."[5] So, traits of character are, for Mandelbaum, essentially dispositional, as opposed to actional, meaning, in his usage, that the actual feelings and motives of a person are relevant to our judgment as to whether he possesses the attribute.[6]

The problem here is again that there does not seem to be a good argument for ruling out, as a part of a person's character, what does not depend so heavily on the motivation of the agent. There seem to be plenty of mediating, aesthetic, meliorating, and instrumental virtues and vices that are not so heavily dependent. More seriously, even when we move to moral virtues and vices, the crucial issues of what is to count as a demand and of what sorts of demands are to count must be faced. There are a great many recurring demands the meeting of which seems to have little to do, on the face of it, with morality. I have suggested a way of setting off one sort of demand—that there be concern for the interests of others or, at least, that there not be the taking of unfair advantage of others—as having particular importance for morality.

Alasdair MacIntyre offers as a 'partial and tentative' definition: ''A virtue is an acquired human quality the possession and exercise of which tends to enable us to achieve those goods which are internal to practices and the lack of which effectively prevents us from achieving any such goods.''[7] While MacIntyre amplifies and extends this definition in ways that I find intriguing, still it has an uncomfortably reductive sound. In the end, it is not clear to me why, given the full spread of what may with justification be counted as virtues, we should be limited to those qualities that have the appropriate relation to the goods that are internal to practices. The distinction between goods external to and internal to a practice is perhaps best indicated by reference to MacIntyre's example of the child, the candy, and chess. A child is motivated by goods external to the practice of chess if he is offered money for candy if he will play to win against an adult who offers the child money and agrees to play in such a way that the child can, with effort, win. This may eventually bring the child to the point that he is able to appreciate and be motivated by the goods that obtain in the playing of chess, ''goods specific to chess, in the achievement of a certain highly particular kind of analytical skill, strategic imagination, and competitive intensity.'' These are goods internal to the practice. While the notion of a practice is a very broad one for MacIntyre, still it is not clear why we should regard that notion as centrally definitive in the concept of a virtue. The issue, to put it in my terms, is whether there should be but one sort of quality, defined by the sort of reason it provides for preference of the bearer, or whether there may not be many sorts, sorts that are mutually irreducible one to another.

The issue between MacIntyre's and my way of understanding virtue is this: MacIntyre's conception takes a particular value as prior. We first determine what is valuable—the values internal to practices—and on that basis determine which qualities are virtues and which are vices. MacIntyre leaves the matter suitably vague by acknowledging that *ex*ternal values also count: the wealth, worldly success, recognition, say, that can result from engaging in practices. The issue, which I would resolve in MacIntyre's favor, of whether internal or external values are most worth cultivating is irrelevant here. (A closer look at that subject would require at least that we distinguish those practices such as the dance or painting, in which external values are a kind of barbarian intrusion, from such practices as the conduct of war or the management of industry, in which the satisfactions gained from the practice are at least arguably secondary to those gained from the consequences of engaging successfully in it.)

On my own (functional) view, we look for those qualities that serve as reasons for preference in the ordinary and not-so-ordinary exigencies of life. Given the fact that much of life, whether in complex or tribal society, consists in engagement in practices, it might seem as if there would be very great overlaps between a functional view and one that makes the status of qualities as virtues contingent on their contribution to the internal values of practices. That may be so, but the basis of designation as a virtue is importantly different. On a functional view, it is the tensions, tendencies, pleasures, and pains of common life, including the engagement in practices, that lead us to value or disvalue this or that quality as responding well or ill to what we go through together. On MacIntyre's view, it is the particular satisfactions of engaging in practices that set off those qualities that are virtues from those that are not. This is, from the functional point of view, so far an arbitrary designation. It is not clear that the value we place on the internal satisfactions of engaging in practices *determines* what is to count as a virtue. As far as I can see, there is no inconsistency in the conjunctive assertion that one holds a given quality to be a virtue but that one does not regard that quality as a necessary or a sufficient condition of enjoying the satisfactions of engaging in a practice or practices.

James Wallace offers a naturalistic conception of virtues and vices.[8] Those qualities are virtues that, roughly, are necessary or desirable for human flourishing, a kind of flourishing that is set off from other kinds primarily by its taking place in convention-governed communities. Vices are qualities that stand in the way of flourishing. Much of what Wallace has to say about flourishing derives from a biological and Aristotelean perspective. What it is for a human to flourish is to be understood in essentially the same way that a biologist determines what it is for a jellyfish or a coyote to flourish. We observe the beings in their typical circumstances of life, and we pick out those who are in some ways unhealthy and abnormal from those who are normal and healthy.

This approach *is* a functional one, a biologically functional one. It recognizes that there can be different qualities that contribute in different ways to human flourishing. At the same time, however, it is observer oriented rather than agent oriented; it is aimed more at explanation than at practical wisdom. The agent, the person living in the convention-ordered community, is not primarily interested in the qualities in other people and in himself that are conducive to or are constitutive of health and flourishing. He is primarily interested in whether he can trust a person, whether he can count on the person's remaining constant in his attitudes, whether he is likely to be cruel or unjust or cowardly. That he would not be cowardly is a good reason to prefer him as a delegate to a bargaining session with the administration; that he is just is a good reason for nominating him to a judgeship. Good character, from the agent's point of view, is not so much character that is seen to be biologically necessary or desirable as it is character that one wants in the choices one must make between persons and also between possible selves. What one wants when one must choose persons may be, in the last analysis, persons whose qualities are necessary for flourishing; but that would remain to be shown.

The class of practically desirable virtues is wider than and is inclusive of the class of virtues necessary for flourishing in any biologically understandable health/normalcy sort of way. There are different conceptions, inevitably, of what it is to flourish, once one moves beyond the biological level. To confine the virtues to the qualities that are conducive to health or normalcy is to suppose that the concern of those people who use the language of virtue is confined or ought to be confined to the commendable ends of encouraging health and normalcy in the human community.

One could go on to an examination of Peter Geach's defense of the traditional narrowing of the frame, or to Philippa Foot's suggestion that virtues are correctives to human nature.[9] But perhaps enough has been said to show that the burden should be on any such reductive definitions to justify the exclusion of wide categories of dispositions that serve as reasons for preference of persons who have them over persons who do not.

Philosophers who would limit the virtues to one or a very few, as Plato and Kant do (and as Aristotle does not), or who would characterize the virtues as dispositions that have this or that function or special character, as many contemporary writers do, are taking the position that only some of what appear to be virtues are indeed virtues. Only some of the apparent grounds for preference and choice of persons are grounds. This is reasonable enough, but what is needed is an argument that the excluded grounds are only apparently such. That is what is lacking in contemporary divisions and what was lacking in much ancient discussion. It is simply not clear why some philosophers should exclude aesthetic or instrumental qualities, for example from virtue, whereas other philosophers would place them stage center. It is this characteristic of discussions of virtue, I think, that alienated most moral philosophers from the ethics of character and that led those psychologists and philosophers who were interested in moral education to ignore what Kohlberg called the 'bag of virtues' approach in favor of emphasis on rules, principles, rights, duties, and obligations.[10]

I have suggested, in this and the previous chapter, that the subject of virtue need not be one that is either arbitrarily simplified or hopelessly amorphous. It is possible to approach the problem of classifying and evaluating the relative weight of virtues by examining the most general grounds on which it is possible to base preference for or avoidance of persons, thinking of persons not as quasi-legal abstractions or causal forces for good or bad but as beings that have certain sorts of disposition. I have also suggested why the 'moral' virtues have seemed especially important to philosophers and educators and why justice has a central place among the moral virtues.

There are, no doubt, many reasons for the relative neglect of the virtues in contemporary ethics. The arbitrariness of definitions of virtue is one reason. Another may be the justified suspicion that virtue ethics is likely to be some form of perfectionism. In the next chapter, I will sketch a form of perfectionism that is consistent with a virtue-oriented approach—a form to which we are naturally led as we attempt to give full weight to virtue considerations. I'll try to show that this form of perfectionism, at least, is not vulnerable to the usual objections.

6

A Defense of Perfectionism

In what follows, I will defend a form of virtue-oriented ethics against criticisms that it is, in some damaging sense, a kind of perfectionism. The thesis I want to defend is that in talk and thought about what ought to be done, there is a certain kind of consideration that governs moral acceptability—a kind that has to do with the virtues and vices. Whether this thesis, more fully made out below, is one that is defensible, all things considered, I do not know and certainly do not try to show here. My objective is merely to show that, although it is perfectionistic in a sense that I will explain, it is a morally defensible form of perfectionism.

Ethical theorists have tended not to pay much attention to a range of considerations that often play a crucial role in reflection, debate, and justification.[1] Quite often, a particular course of action or a policy is characterized as unkind, cowardly, cruel, dishonest, vindictive, unjust, disloyal, or selfish. These terms, plus a few more, and their positive counterparts—kind, honest, and so on—form a class, the size of which is indefinitely, but not very, large. Let us call this class the class of virtue and vice considerations. Each such consideration points to a particular quality of an act or policy, a quality that makes the doing of (or the agreeing to) it morally desirable or morally questionable. The introduction of a virtue consideration (for short) has a tendency to give shape to the subsequent discussion, since it introduces rules of relevance. Thus, to say of a proposal to sell sophisticated

I should like to thank Robert Simon and John Moskop for their comments on the first draft of the chapter.

arms to Taiwan that it would be disloyal to Mainland China is to introduce a line of discussion that will focus on rather different, primarily historical, considerations than would have been relevant if the contention had been that the policy was dishonest. That discussion, in turn, would be a different one from the discussion of whether selling arms to Taiwan would be an unfair policy with respect to Mainland China or that it would be a cowardly policy or a merely selfish one. The discussion of whether an action or a policy is morally acceptable or unacceptable often turns on such considerations. These considerations have claim, at the least, to being weighty ones in moral discourse, as can be seen by reflecting on their relation to ones having to do with rights and duties.

Suppose it is contended that Mainland China has a right that we not sell arms to Taiwan. This contention appeals either to a supposed or to an actual network of rights and duties that result from agreed upon or understood rules or principles that govern relations between us and Mainland China or between nations generally. But in addition to the question of whether a right would be violated, there is the question of what the moral import would be of violating the right. This is a question that turns back on the agent, so to speak, and critically probes his motives. To violate the right of Mainland China might be morally more acceptable if at the same time the policy is what loyalty to Taiwan requires or if the policy is motivated by concern for the well-being of Taiwan, supposing that Taiwan is under a threat of invasion. To admit to violating a right is to concede that one has the burden of moral proof in adopting the course of action in question; but the admission does not dispose of the problem of what to do. It does not dispose of the problem because what is still at issue is what morally follows, if we do what it is proposed that we should do. We do not want to do what is cruel, unjust, cowardly, disloyal, and so forth. But if, on the other hand, none of this were to follow, if no virtue considerations could be brought to bear adversely on the course of action, then, even though a right is being violated, the course of action is morally permissible. Rights talk, in short, must be qualified by the sort of talk we engage in when we make use of virtue considerations.

It is possible, then, to hold a weak thesis to the effect that virtue considerations have weight, that they cannot be ignored, or that they qualify in some way the moral acceptability of a proposed action or policy. Or a stronger thesis can be maintained to the effect that they govern moral acceptability. I will defend the stronger thesis against 'perfectionist' criticisms. To say that virtue considerations govern acceptability is to say that it is a necessary and sufficient condition of the moral acceptability of an action or a course of action that it not violate the requirements of the relevant set of virtue considerations. The 'not violating' of those requirements is a relative matter. It may be that some balancing of the considerations must be done: some may have to give way, more or less, to others. In the happy circumstances when there is no conflict between virtue considerations with respect to a course of action, we may say that the course of action or the policy is the one that is fully acceptable. Thus, to show that it is morally fully acceptable that we sell sophisticated arms to Taiwan, we would have to show that there are no relevant virtue considerations that oppose it and that the relevant considerations approve it. Needless to say, it is difficult to show that a course of action is fully acceptable, and we may more typically have to settle for trying to show that it is acceptable—that, for example, even though the policy is arguably a bit unfair to the People's Republic of China, it is required by loyalty to Taiwan and by the sense that not to supply Taiwan with what would prevent its being invaded would be callous and, given the history of our relationships, ungrateful.

In what sense is the thesis that virtue considerations govern the moral acceptability of actions or policies ('the Thesis' for short) a perfectionistic one? Perfectionistic theories cover a very wide range. They differ on the criteria of perfection, on who or what is to be perfected, on who is to do the perfecting, and on how the perfecting is to be accomplished. Not only may the criteria of excellence in which perfection is thought to exist differ, but the height of the standards of excellence may vary. The legendary honesty of Lincoln may set a higher standard of honest behavior than that set by the average professor of philosophy. Perfectionistic doctrines may have primarily or exclusively to do with the perfection of the agent or of some group or of everyone in general.[2] The agent of perfection may be a person or a group or everyone or God. And perfection may be brought about in a variety of ways.

I will take it that moral perfectionism, in its most general form, as it bears on actions and policies, is the doctrine that the overall acceptability or unacceptability of an action or policy is to be determined by the extent to which the action or policy accords with standards of excellence.[3] That is a sufficiently general understanding to incorporate the differences in criteria, objects, agents, and means of perfection that I have mentioned. To say that virtue considerations govern moral acceptability is, then, a perfectionistic position. It may not be the most general perfectionistic position, since other criteria are imaginable; but it is very wide and open. It does not insist that any particular moral criterion—for example, justice—has sole claim to relevance when the question is what ought to be done. And it posits no hierarchical relations between the criteria, or considerations, whose relevance it maintains.

No ethical theory that I know of rules out virtue considerations as being relevant to moral decision or justification; but they may be systematically relegated to the periphery of moral thought. This may happen by making them conceptually vacuous, as deriving all of their force from 'more fundamental' conceptions: rules, principles, rights, and duties. Or it may happen by promoting virtue considerations to the region of the supererogatory, a region that has to do, not with what is morally most significant, but with what is a kind of moral luxury: the admirable-if-it-occurs. A reason for relegating virtue considerations to the periphery may be the justified suspicion that they are perfectionistic, combined with the unjustified notion that perfectionistic considerations should not have a place at the center of moral concern. They should yield that place to sterner matters, matters that have to do, not with what would be more or less perfect, but with what is required of us, as morally mandatory. Achieving excellence, it might be thought, is fine enough, but we may pursue it with a clear conscience only after we have attended to our duties and met our obligations. What those are is the first and fundamental question. Let me sketch an alternative way of thinking about the weight of moral considerations.

As a preliminary, let me remark that in thinking about excellence, we must also think about the absence of excellence and the various ways in which we can be far from excellence. We can say that an act is a courageous or loyal thing to do only against a background understanding of what it is for an act to be cowardly or disloyal, so that we can think of courageous acts as having a preferred place on a continuum that leads all the way from 'cowardly' to 'indifferent' to 'courageous'. So we must not think that a consideration's being perfectionistic amounts only to its being concerned with the attainment of the high end of the scale. It may also have to do with the low end—with not doing what is morally to be avoided. Perfectionistic considerations should not, then, be regarded as being concerned only with moral luxuries, with pictures of ideal behavior, or with the emulation of ideal moral models. This is not at all to rule out the relevance to moral deliberation and justification of such notions; but it is to say that if the objection to perfectionism is that it is only concerned with this end of the continuum, then the objection is misconceived; it fails to find the mark.

One way to assess the weight of moral considerations is to think not so much in terms merely of what I ought to do simpliciter, what my rights and duties are, but of what I would be by doing or agreeing to a given thing. What has weight with me is what I think of myself as being. This is the side of moral deliberation that tends to be overlooked or underplayed by contemporary ethical theories. If I do not care what I am or am becoming, whether I am fair or unfair, cruel or kind, honest or dishonest, then moral talk will have little significance for me. To whatever extent I have moral standards or ideals, to whatever extent I have aversions to selves that I could become, I will find virtue considerations weighty.

Virtue considerations are sometimes thought of as moral principles—for example, by Geoffrey Warnock.[4] But the way in which they function as principles must be set off rather carefully from the way in which some other sorts of principles operate. The point to notice is that these principles are substantive, in the sense that living by them is conceptually tied to being a certain sort of person, where the sort in question is morally significant. It will be helpful to contrast the principle that one should do what is required by a virtue consideration with the principle that one should so act as to maximize happiness and minimize misery. The latter principle can be adopted out of a variety of motives. A person may hope to gain glory by increasing the general happiness or power or the love of the populace. He will be nonetheless an effective advocate of the principle for any of that. The principle that one should act in this happiness-maximizing way should be distinguished from the principle that one should be benevolent toward others. Aside from the points that the happiness-maximizing principle is understood and advocated as the sole principle that ought to govern action and that the benevolence principle generally is not, there is the less-often-noted point that benevolence has to do with a particular kind of motive and happiness maximizing does not.

The argument has often been offered against utilitarianism that if the public happiness is taken as the sole end, a variety of morally questionable means could be used to achieve it: for example, the enslavement of a minority, the punishment of the innocent, or sub-rosa coercion. What should also be apparent is that being a good utilitarian is consistent with being a morally undesirable sort of person. It is not necessarily the case that the person who wants and strives for the general happiness is therefore benevolent. He could even be misanthropic and, in some Kafka-like scenario, think that by increasing the general average happiness, he will at the same time be contributing to the general decline of humanity and to its disappearance from the face of the earth.[5]

A parallel point can be made about being a formalist, the sort of Kantian who insists on the first formulation of the categorical imperative and forgets the second. The first formulation, which has to do solely with the consistency of self-legislated universal rules, can be adhered to by a person of vile moral character who happens at the same time to be consistent—consistently vile. The second formulation, on the other hand, comes close to being a virtue consideration. It would be so if it told us to be respectful of other people, to be concerned about them, to have that motive in our dealings with them. Perhaps that is what Kant means. I think that it is. But he says to treat everyone, including ourselves, as ends in themselves and never merely as means. While it may require a stretch of the imagination, it is still conceivable that even this principle could be obeyed for the wrong motives and by a person whose moral character is far from desirable. A person might treat others and himself as ends in themselves without any deeper concern for them or for himself than that he thought that was what was required of him by God (or perhaps by the ghost of Kant). He could even think that the treating of persons as ends in themselves was commanded by Satan, whom he worships and feels bound to obey, but who has malevolent intentions toward the human race. He could treat people as ends in themselves out of a sort of moral ennui in which he picks up that principle as no more tiring than the others that are offered to him.

But let us return to the question of whether the contention that virtue considerations govern moral acceptability (the Thesis) is a defensible form of moral perfectionism. In pursuing that question, I will take up three forms, or varieties, of perfectionism, corresponding to the chief objections to an undifferentiated 'perfectionism': Brittle Perfectionism, Arbitrary Perfectionism, and Spiritual Egotism. These are, respectively, theories that require the attainment of an impossible ideal of perfection, theories that arbitrarily impose standards of perfection on persons who have a right to choose their own standards, and theories that emphasize a kind of psyche polishing that can rightly be regarded as a form of egotism. My conclusion will be not only that the Thesis has no necessary connection with theories of these kinds but also that it is a mistake to confuse the Thesis with any of these forms of perfectionism. The Thesis is, just the same, a perfectionistic one.

The advocate of the Thesis is not, of course, committed to the view that we must, on pain of some kind of moral failing, attain *perfect* honesty, justice, courage, or loyalty. It is nevertheless worth exploring Brittle Perfectionism a little so as to point up the ease with which one could come to think of the Thesis as a form of Brittle Perfectionism.[6] To begin with, we should notice that it is not really clear what kind of impossibility is in question when it is said that it is impossible to attain perfect honesty or justice. Why is it *impossible* to attain perfect honesty, say? Is the impossibility in question an empirical one, a conceptual one, or some other kind? Is it so *difficult* to attain perfect honesty that we can never quite manage it, or is 'perfect honesty' an incoherent notion, so that we don't know what it would mean to attain it? With respect to empirical impossibility, trying to be honest *does* seem to be like trying to overcome 'real', not conceptual, difficulties. We can recognize that it is not enough to tell the truth in everyday contexts, not to filch from the cash register, or not to cheat at poker. We could pass these tests and still not be honest. But why is this so? Why is it hard, perhaps impossible, to be *completely* honest? It seems that no matter what we do or don't do, the question can still be asked whether we could not be more honest than we are.

The answer might be given that honesty is an open-textured concept: no formula will provide, in the end, all of the requirements for being honest. If we say that being honest is being open and undeceptive, then the problem descends to the question of what it is to be open and undeceptive. And if we offer formulae for those notions, the terms used in the formulae will be found to be open-textured too. We cannot find the end of that road. But is not our problem a general one? Very many of the terms in natural language are open-textured. Questions can be raised about what really is a mountain or a desk, as well as about what really is justice or honesty. If our problem is a special case of the general problem that many of the terms of natural language are open-textured, then it is not a problem that should disturb us. For just as we have no problem in deciding that the Rockies are mountains, we have no trouble in deciding that Lincoln was honest. Honest people are people who behave honestly, and we can ''go on from there.'' By pointing to the open texture of virtue terms, we have not explained just why or in what sense it is very hard to fulfill the requirements of justice, honesty, or courage.

It is not a problem of open texture, but of 'high redefinition' that makes perfect honesty impossible to attain. No matter what even an Abe Lincoln does in trying to be honest, he can still ask himself whether he is being truly honest. This is so because no matter what standards he attains, the standards can always be cranked up another notch, so that he can never reach *the* highest standard. Jones's maximal honesty—paying debts and telling the truth—may be Smith's minimal honesty, and Smith's minimal standard may fall below Green's minimal standard. The open question, then, is a question of the relative height of standards. If, in principle, the standard can always be set higher than 'the top' standard, perfection can never be attained. Brittle Perfectionism thus requires the attainment of what it is impossible to attain. Since, however, the advocate of the Thesis need not also be engaged in the business of meeting the requirements of an ever-receding top standard, the Thesis is not a form of Brittle Perfectionism.

The second theory-defining objection, which defines Arbitrary Perfectionism, is that the standard of perfection is set by fiat, without regard for reasoned objections. Arbitrary Perfectionism would, presumably, attempt to regiment everyone under the banners of some improvement campaign to which people in a free society need not agree: a puritanical community, say, or a community of stoics or one of saints.

The question is whether the Thesis, by insisting that virtue considerations govern, becomes or in some way invites Arbitrary Perfectionism. This raises, in turn, the question of whether appeals to honesty, justice, and so forth, invoke arbitrary standards, standards that can then only be imposed on everyone by fiat. In approaching the issue, it is useful to bear in mind a distinction. The Thesis does not hold that any particular act or policy is morally acceptable or unacceptable. It holds, rather, that to justify choice or rejection, one must show that the choice or rejection accords with the requirements of the virtue considerations. Therefore the Thesis is perfectionistic at the level of criteria of justification, rather than at the level of choice or decision. It is, thus, not an objection to the Thesis that it would or would not approve of this or that choice.

Rawls's objection to perfectionism is to the effect that there is no "agreed criterion of perfection that can be used as a principle for choosing between institutions" and that, hence, there can be no ground, consistent with justice, for people to "use the coercive apparatus of the state to win for themselves a greater liberty or larger distributive shares on the grounds that their activities are of more intrinsic value." Thus, "Perfectionism is denied [to persons in the original position] as a political principle."[7]

There are, as several writers have seen,[8] important problems for Rawls's contract theory in his rejection of appeals to principles of perfection in the original position. To take up that issue here would be digressive. Yet it is worth showing that the Rawlsian reservations about perfectionism do not depreciate the credentials of the Thesis. The perfectionism of the Thesis has to do with criteria that do have strong claim not to be arbitrary. Where does the burden of proof lie if the claim is made that appeals to honesty, kindness, loyalty, or nonselfishness are arbitrary? Indeed, there may be arbitrarily demanding standards of honesty, say; but it does not follow that raising the question of whether an action or policy is honest amounts in itself to the imposition of an arbitrary standard. There is, in this sense, a nonarbitrary criterion of perfection that, with other such criteria, governs the moral acceptability of acts and policies.

The peculiarity of choices between possible *institutions* (Rawls's problem) is that—as opposed to choices of acts and policies, in which designatable persons are affected—only one of the virtue considerations is clearly applicable: namely, justice. It would be more than odd to speak of the honesty or loyalty of an institution. Acts and policies are things that we do or undertake. They can be done or undertaken honestly or out of loyalty. Institutions are conceptually impersonal, in that they have no owners, correspond to no agents, and have no place in time or space. They are arrangements of rules and roles that we may or may not decide to adopt. They can, in fairly or unfairly distributing benefits and burdens, be just or unjust; but they cannot be honest or loyal. In adopting an institution, we are (ideally—and that is the point of the original position) not doing anything to or about any particular persons. But to say that an act or policy is honest or loyal is to imply that there is some particular person with respect to whom it is honest or loyal.

An example of Arbitrary Perfectionism is the theory that speaks of the 'real nature' of human beings as something that we must strive toward. This is to introduce a supposed standard under which it is possible to list just those qualities that the writer or speaker approves as virtues. The notion may be, as in Saint Thomas, that we have a God-given nature that we must do our best to attain. It may be that we are urged, as by Epictetus, to "follow our natures." Or it may be that, in some inverted sense of moral perfection, following our natures becomes, as for Freud, the attainment of an ideal of mental health. Self-realizational ethics, too, may provide us with examples of Arbitrary Perfectionism, since the choice between possible selves to be realized may be an arbitrary one.[9]

It could be argued that arbitrariness is inevitable in insisting that virtue considerations govern the acceptability of actions and policies, since that insistence amounts to saying that the action or policy that is worthy of choice is the one that approximates most closely to a certain arbitrarily chosen *ideal*. The ideal is, so it might be thought, a certain pattern of virtues in action or policy. It must be an arbitrarily chosen pattern, since there is no general agreement on which pattern is most desirable. Whichever pattern we choose is, thus, chosen arbitrarily and becomes the ideal against which we measure the moral acceptability or unacceptability of the act or policy. However, this argument presupposes, falsely, that to say of an action or policy that it is the alternative most favored by the virtue considerations is to appeal tacitly to some ideal pattern of virtues. It does not follow from the admission of multiple criteria of assessment—the virtue considerations—that there is some preferred pattern, an ideal, that must be exemplified by that which is chosen. It is possible to honor virtue in the absence of a picture of some ideal model of action toward which we must move. One need not have any such ideal in order to assess actions and policies along the different parameters of justice, loyalty, noncruelty, and so on.[10]

I turn now to the third theory-defining objection to perfectionism: that it is what John Dewey calls 'spiritual egotism'. "Some," Dewey says, "are preoccupied with the state of their character, concerned for the purity of their motives and the goodness of their souls. The exultation of conceit which sometimes accompanies this absorption can produce a corrosive inhumanity which exceeds the possibilities of any other known form of selfishness."[11]

One kind of spiritual egotist, Dewey might agree, is the 'moral athlete' approved by James Walker, Francis Wayland, and other nineteenth-century textbook writers.[12] Some of these earnest men convey a picture of the world as an arena in which people are engaged in the testing of virtue, like athletes striving for the greatest distance or the fastest time. Another sort of spiritual egotist is the perfectionist who regards detachment from political affairs as a necessary condition of the attainment of his ideal. Thomas Upham, one of these textbook writers, advises those of his readers who want to achieve a "holy and upright life" to "stand aloof from the tactics of party, and whatever constitutes the machinery of party movement." The Christian citizen must, on Upham's view, avoid means that "do not commend themselves to the spirit of perfect rectitude."[13]

The charge of 'spiritual egotism', if well founded, converts an apparent advantage of the Thesis into a disadvantage. An apparent advantage of the Thesis over other conceptions of what it is to justify a moral conclusion is that it bridges the supposed gap between the description of an act or policy and the conclusion that it ought to be done or adopted. It performs this feat, supposedly, by describing the feat in such a way—for example, as dishonest—that if I do it, I am to that extent dishonest. But since I ought not do what is dishonest, I ought not do this act. It also bridges a supposed gap between 'cognition' and motivation, since in coming to know that the act would be dishonest, I come to know that it is something I do not want to do, given that I do not want to be a person of bad character, that is, a person who is not worthy of preference by others.[14] But this double gap-bridging feat can be looked at in another way, the way in which the Deweyan critic might look at it. For he can say that the gaps may be bridged only because my whole moral orientation is askew. In thinking about whether what I am doing is truly honest or kind, I could be concerned just with the perfecting of my own image. I could be a narcissistic moral preener whose motivation is thus morally questionable. The virtue considerations bridge the gap, if they do, because they supposedly look both ways at once. They apply both to me and to the act that I propose to do. If the act has a certain characteristic, then, thus far, I have that characteristic if I do it: if it is kind, I am thus far kind. What, then, is my motivation? Is it to have that characteristic, or is it to do an act that has that characteristic? If it is to have that characteristic—kindness, say—then what is the source of that motive, the motive to do what is kind? Is it a morally defensible motive, or is it pride in the portrait of perfection that I am thereby touching up?

Another way to pose the issue is by drawing a contrast between 'self-regarding' and 'other-regarding' considerations. Is the point that what I propose to do is dishonest a remark about what I would be if I were to do it or about the effect that it would have on other people if I did it? To whatever extent it is self-regarding, Dewey could hold, it presents a morally suspect, because possibly 'spiritually egotistic', reason for doing the act.

What defense of the Thesis can be offered, then, against the charge that it is a form of 'spiritual egotism'? The answer is reasonably clear, once the charge is understood. For the charge amounts to this: that whoever holds that the virtue considerations govern moral acceptability of what we ought to do runs a certain *danger.* He can come to make the virtue considerations the accomplices of a morally repugnant way of thinking. Instead of thinking simply what is the honest or kind or just thing to do, he can think whether by doing the proposed act, he will embellish his character in this or that way. He is concerned to polish up his attainments of justice, honesty, or kindness so that he can be satisfied with the image of self that he then sees. He will *do* what is honest, and so forth, but his motives will be narcissistic ones.

The answer is that the seen danger is a real danger, that we should be on our guard against it, that we should be continually aware of it. It is, however, far from a necessary consequence of accepting the Thesis that one must fall victim to 'spiritual egotism'. Even though the virtue considerations may *seem* to be inherently self-regarding, even though arguing that if I did this or that, I would be being cruel may *seem* to be taking too much interest in my own moral image, there is no necessary narcissistic self-regarding interpretation, no necessity for image burnishing. A more straightforward interpretation is that what is wrong is not that the act would put blotches and smears on the escutcheon of my character, thus ruining the picture of perfection, but that what I propose to do is wrong because it would be cruel to someone. The reflection that a given act would be cruel is no more inherently self-regarding than it is other-regarding. The interesting thing about the virtue considerations it that it is both.

Have I, in this sketch of possible objections to the Thesis as a form of perfectionism, overlooked some underlying source of uncomfortableness with the Thesis's perfectionistic tendency? Perhaps I have. But I think that the chief source of uncomfortableness with perfectionism as an ethical theory is with the amorphousness of the theory, the sense that it can take shapes that we would do well to shy away from. And I have tried to show that Thesis perfectionism does not necessarily have the most repugnant of those shapes. Yet it is a perfectionistic theory. It insists that the moral acceptability of actions or policies turns entirely on the extent to which they approximate the requirements of a set of standards: the closer the approximation, the more preferable the act or policy. The standards set by a perfectionistic theory need not be impossible of attainment, arbitrarily imposed, or made use of in morally questionable ways. These are simply dangers that must be avoided by those who believe, as I suspect, that the virtue considerations constitute the set of standards that govern moral acceptability.

7

Ideals of Virtue and Moral Obligation: Gandhi

From the point of view of consequential, formal, or contract theories, appeals to personal ideals may be suspect. It may be argued that such ideals are idiosyncratic and unstable. No one else can hold me responsible if I do not live up to them. They are mine to make and to violate. The 'duties' to which ideals give rise are therefore optional, as genuine moral duties are not. There is no optionality in moral duties; but ideal-derived duties last only so long as I hold to the ideals that undergird them. Moral duties are categorically incumbent upon me; changing my ideals will not rid me of them.

A second, related, criticism is that considerations that have to do with personal ideals and with moving toward or sliding away from them are self-regarding, whereas 'genuine' moral considerations are other-regarding. The implication is that to follow a personal moral ideal and to measure one's moral progress against it must constitute a form of narcissistic selfishness, a turning away from one's moral ties to others. It is to imply that the very adoption of a personal moral ideal is morally questionable, leading to undue preoccupation with one's own development, a kind of moral preening, when one should simply be doing what is right because one has an obligation to do so.

I am especially grateful to James Wallace and Kurt Baier for their criticisms of an earlier version of this chapter. The first (and now remote) ancestor of this essay appeared as "Selves, Ideals, and Others: The Example of Gandhi," in *The Individual and Society: Essays Presented to David L. Miller*, ed. Michael P. Jones et al. (Southwestern Journal of Philosophy, 1978).

In what follows, I will argue that the distinction between self-regarding and other-regarding considerations is not as easy to make as is often supposed and that even when it can be made with some assurance, it is not clear that moral considerations fall uniformly on the other-regarding side of the line. At the same time, I want to find the center of gravity of the objection to including personal ideals as matters of some weight in making moral decisions. To prevent the argument from becoming excessively abstract, I will focus on the complex moral ideals of an arguably moral man: Mohandas Gandhi.

I do not mean to argue *for* Gandhi's ideals, but just to take them as a clear example *of* ideals and to point to Gandhi's life as an example (dramatic to be sure) of an ideal-inspired life. My overall objective, one that I can do no more than indicate here, is to show how spare and sere, how unjustifiably reductivist is an ethics that confines itself to questions of what sort of acts are right and what sort wrong, what kinds of things we may or may not do, what duties there are, and what obligations. For the reflective agent there is, I want to say, always the subjective side of these questions: the concern with the sort of person one has been, is, and is becoming; the sense of direction or the lack of it; the strengthening or weakening of will; the cultivation of sympathy; the encouragement of imagination; the life plans, however vague; the moral models and their shifting roles; the self-and-other assessment against the very many scales that are available to use through the language of virtue and vice.

A moral problem can as well concern conflicts among one's ideals and between one's ideals and one's duties as it can concern the question of what one's duties and obligations are.

We know of the special place that the "Vaishnava Janas," a fifteenth-century song, had for Gandhi. It was an expression of what, in his conception, it meant to be a true follower of Vishnu.

He is the true Vaishnava who knows and feels another's woes as his own. Ever ready to serve, he never boasts.

He bows to everyone and despises no one, keeping his thought, word and deed pure. . . .

He looks upon all with an equal eye. He has rid himself of lust. . . .

His tongue would fail him if he attempted to utter an untruth.

He covets not another's wealth. . . .

He has conquered greed, hypocrisy, passion, and anger.[1]

It is well known that Gandhi was one who "knows and feels another's woes as his own" and he was "ever ready to serve" in the cause of the removal of those woes. It is also well known that Gandhi was concerned about conquering himself: his lust, greed, hypocrisy, passion, and anger. There were bound to arise times when serving came into conflict with self-conquering.

The urge to conquer himself led Gandhi into a variety of ascetic practices, including fasts. The fasts were typically for political ends, in the interest of those who "had woes," but they also served personal ends, the purification of the self and the achievement of the vision of God. Especially in his later years, it was hard to say which ends predominated. Gandhi believed that there was no conflict, since he held that the example of a "pure man" could be tremendously efficacious in the world; and he felt that by "purifying himself and subjugating the flesh he would increase the powers of the soul and thus acquire the strength to dominate events" (*LDM*, 557). But on the part of Gandhi's friends and critics, the question inevitably arose, which end was foremost. Was Gandhi primarily interested in self-purification or in the vision of God; or was his primary interest in removing the British administration from India? If the attainment of self-purification was instrumental to power in the world, then the worst that Gandhi might have been accused of was that by fasting, he was sharpening his spiritual weapons when he should have been using them. But if the intrinsically valuable purified self was his primary aim, then he was open to the charge that he was allowing purely personal, even selfish, aims to interfere with the attainment of public ends to which he was publicly committed and to which he had been the cause of others' committal. The latter charge is the more serious, but whether it or the former is true is beside the point. We merely want to see a nexus in Gandhi's life where considerations of different sorts come to bear.

Perhaps enough has already been set before us so that we can begin to be aware of how very facile it is to speak as if there were a straight line between other-regarding and self-regarding considerations. If by 'self-regarding' is meant 'having regard to one's own ideals of perfection', then *all* of the injunctions of the "Vaishnava Janas" are self-regarding, for they all express aspects of the ideal Vaishnava, which Gandhi aspired to become. But at the same time, parts of this ideal specifically enjoin service to others and lay upon one duties toward others.

I have now spoken of conflicts latent within Gandhi's ideal. Before passing to the subject of conflicts between that ideal and duties and obligations incumbent upon Gandhi,[2] it may be useful to take advantage, in passing, of the light that the "Vaishnava Janas" can throw on the concept of a moral consideration. Contemplation of the ideal and of the role that it played in Gandhi's life should make us aware of a certain lameness in the very notion of a 'consideration'. It would be ridiculous to suppose that every time Gandhi was faced with a moral dilemma he made use of some such formula as, "To do X would be hypocritical, and therefore I may not do it, since to do so would be unworthy of a true Vaishnava." In short, references to his moral ideal would have seemed stilted, even uncomfortably priggish. It would therefore be wrong to read 'considerations' narrowly, as applying only to what the agent may bring explicitly to bear as a reason for or against a line of action. But if we interpret 'considerations' more generously, to include everything that the agent takes into account in arriving at his decisions, then surely the ideal pattern that the agent sets for himself is a matrix of moral considerations. The ideal is not revealed on every occasion; but its influence on thought and action is nevertheless evident; and it can be alluded to by remarks about what one may and may not permit oneself to do, when critics press for justification.

Now let us turn to conflicts that arose between Gandhi's ideals and his non-ideal-related duties. I shall mention the frictions that developed between Gandhi's duties to his wife and his fellow citizens and two different sorts of ideals—moral and spiritual. The moral ideal that is contained, like the spiritual one, in the "Vaishnava Janas" is to be of service to those experiencing 'woes'. It is an ideal of dedication to a cause—the well-being of the worst off; and it is at the same time an ideal of character—that he should shape himself into an effective instrument for the cause. The spiritual ideal is to attain and to live in the vision of God. It is an ideal of the attainment of a particular state, for which the required changes are not so much character changes as a transformation of the self into a new kind of being. We will turn first, then, to conflicts between moral ideals and duties.

Gandhi's life was so dedicated to the service of his fellow Indians in South Africa that Kasturbhai, his wife, had to wait three years in India before he was ready to bring her to South Africa. On arrival, she found her house full of law clerks, whom she had to look after, in addition to her family; and Gandhi even went so far as to bring a leper into the house in the hope of curing him (*LDM*, 117). Kasturbhai rebelled, and Gandhi regarded the rebellion as nonsense. When Kasturbhai became seriously ill while Gandhi was in jail in Volksrust, he wrote a letter to her in which he assured her that even if she should die, her death would be a sacrifice to the cause of passive resistance, that it did not matter much whether one lived or died in the struggle, and that he hoped she would agree (*LDM*, 192–93). All of this time, he could have walked out of jail without posting bond. It was not until two weeks after his release, with her condition still most serious, that he felt free to hurry to her bedside.

In later life, Gandhi came to change his ideas about the status of women and thus to bring into question the relationship that had existed with Kasturbhai. But even given the status of women in Indian culture, there had been a question all along as to whether he was not deficient in his duties to Kasturbhai, sacrificing her interests and well-being to his ideals of duty to those who had 'woes'.

Gandhi's interest in those who had woes was not confined to their material well-being; it also extended to their, and everyone else's, spiritual well-being. It was in the interest of everyone, he felt, to attain to a kind of simple purity that he tried to exhibit in his own life. The question inevitably arose as to whether, given his enormous influence and the uses he made of it, he was sacrificing India to those ideals. For example, in his debate with Margaret Sanger, it became apparent that Gandhi was willing to risk a continued acceleration in population growth in India if the only effective countermeasure was the use of contraceptives, which Gandhi considered to be incompatible with the pure life. Again, he became convinced that ''increase of material comforts . . . does not in any way conduce to moral growth,'' and on this ground and under Tolstoy's influence, he was led to reject all of the work of modern industrial civilization, including textile mills, railways, telegraph service, lawyers, doctors, and hospitals, in favor of the ''simple peasant life'' (*LDM*, 216). Gandhi was accustomed to taking charge of the spiritual development of his family, the ashramites, and the fellow workers in revolutionary causes; and it seemed but a natural extension, when all of India was his follower, to take charge of the spiritual development of India.

The difficulty, then, was not only that Gandhi was himself torn between his duties to his family and followers, on the one hand, and his ideals of personal moral and spiritual development, on the other, although this no doubt occurred. The difficulty was also that Gandhi's friends and critics were torn by their intuition that Gandhi sometimes gave short shrift to his duties on the unwarranted assumption that his family and friends shared his personal ideals and could expect to be governed by him in their name. Such judgments are especially difficult when they concern a man who is not only himself a person of sharply defined ideals but one who is at the same time a moral and spiritual leader. For it then is sometimes difficult to distinguish occasions on which the interests of his family and friends were sacrificed, given that they were not imbued with Gandhi's ideals, and occasions on which their interests were not sacrificed, since the privations and disappointments that Gandhi inflicted on them were in the name of a shared ideal. Once again, the distinction between other- and self-regarding considerations is not a straightforward one. It is especially difficult to sort out the self-regarding aspects of 'ideal' considerations from the non-self-regarding aspects. In one sense, every reference to a personal ideal is self-regarding. But we have now seen that there may be ambiguities in the status of an ideal, between its being a merely personal or a communal one.

Nevertheless, it does seem to be the case, once these ambiguities are sorted out, that there can be conflicts between Gandhi the father, husband, and friend (i.e., between the duties incumbent upon him in these capacities) and Gandhi the individual concerned with attaining the requirements of a demanding ideal. What is at issue is whether, in such conflicts, the only 'truly moral' considerations are those that have to do with 'external' duties, rather than with 'self-imposed' and perhaps 'arbitrary' ideals of personal character. Does not the idealist bump his head against moral reality upon occasion? Surely he is not free to create his own moral world.

B efore taking up these questions directly and now that we have the example of Gandhi before us, let us set aside some possible confusions. The first of these is to suppose that the distinguishing characteristic of other-regarding considerations is that they have to do with the 'external' or 'publicly observable' aspects of a man's behavior, whereas self-regarding considerations concern 'internal' and 'private' behavior. As we have seen, it would be difficult to say of any of the qualities of character mentioned in the "Vaishnava Janas" that it is exclusively self- or other-regarding. But suppose that the critic grants this and raises the question of whether when a quality is considered as referring to one's relations with other people, it may not be easily distinguishable from the quality that goes by the same name when considered as referring to oneself. Thus, the avoidance of the vice of lust is enjoined. Is the avoidance of lust a self-regarding obligation, having to do with an ideal of behavior; or is it an obligation owed to other persons? In its former aspect, it might be held, what is at issue is solely the individual's private, his nonpublic, behavior; in the latter, his public behavior is at issue. Obligation has to do with behavior toward others, and, so the position goes, this is public; but it does not have to do with the 'internal' behavior of oneself toward oneself.

The analogy with the law—the criminal law—is apparent. The community has the right, it will be said, to demand that certain standards be met in the public behavior of its citizens. They may not kill, rob, molest, or in other ways harm one another. But the law does not, as the voice of the community, have anything to say about the purely private life of its members. Each may think his own thoughts and entertain whatever desires he wants in private. Similarly with 'true' moral obligations: they have to do with the rights of others that the individual not engage in activity that is in some way against their interest. But the analogy breaks down. First of all, the law is not concerned solely with activities that harm others. There are, arguably, 'victimless' crimes, for example the possession of drugs in noncommercial quantities. Secondly, there are generally recognized moral obligations, such as gratitude, that are not fit subjects for legislation. More directly to the point, we cannot legislate against lust, even considered as a public and other-regarding offense. A person's lust may be evident, public; but its prohibition might require instruments of control that would be morally unacceptable. In general, the legal principle that there must be an act for the existence of a crime (which has large exceptions) does not translate easily into a principle of moral life.

There is a sense of the term 'self-regarding' in which the thesis that self-regarding duties cannot be moral ones is not only plausible but is also patently true. In this sense, to say of a duty that it is self-regarding is not to say that it derives from some ideal standard that one sets for oneself but that it is not really a duty at all, merely the quasi-legal mask for a purely selfish desire. Thus, a man might hold it to be his duty to himself to falsify his tax return on the ground that other people do it and that if he does not, he will be at a competitive disadvantage. This is not a duty at all, even though the circumstances might be such that he would be financially ruined if he did not follow the policy of falsification. It is not the case that he is setting ideal standards for his behavior which are above or beyond the common standards by which all must abide; but it is the case that he is participating in the general destruction of standards. Standards do not really come into it, from his point of view. He could not plead this 'duty' as ground for abrogating a duty. In philosophical theory, such considerations are often referred to as 'prudential', and the tacit assumption is that not only are all selfish considerations prudential, but all prudential considerations are selfish. This leads to yet more confusion in the discussion of self-regarding duties and personal moral ideals.

For an accusation of selfishness, it is not sufficient ground that a person is looking out for his own interests. It was not selfishness on Gandhi's part when, discovering that his legal education would cost more than he had thought, he wrote from London to the British agent for Porbandar that he needed four hundred more pounds to complete his legal education. To be selfish, one must look out for one's own interest to the detriment of the interest of others. Ayn Rand practices sophistry when she asserts, on the first page of the Introduction to *The Virtue of Selfishness* that "the exact meaning and dictionary definition of the word 'selfishness' is" *concern with one's own interest.*[3]

Prudent people, as opposed to selfish ones, "apply a habitual deliberateness, caution, and circumspection in action."[4] The considerations of prudence, then, have to do with the best (the most effective, cautious, successful in the past, least dangerous) way to go about getting something done. But not all considerations of prudence are self-regarding. Reflective men of action must necessarily take into account considerations of prudence in a world in which thinking does not make it so. A prudent engineer or economist is much to be preferred to an imprudent one. But of course a person can be prudent or imprudent in his private affairs as well. He can live within his income, insist on a competent survey of property that he is considering for purchase, and see to it that his sons and daughters acquire the educational requisites for livelihood. In arguing that not all self-regarding considerations are prudential, I do not depreciate prudential considerations. Gandhi's moral character is not diminished by his having had the foresight to request additional funds for his legal education before he reached the end of his resources. But if self-regarding considerations can be moral ones, as I want to show, it is necessary to argue that they are not necessarily prudential.

For Gandhi, whatever distance he could travel toward becoming a 'true Vaishnava' was intrinsically worthwhile. He was not, in striving toward those ideals, ''applying a habitual deliberateness, caution, and circumspection in action.'' If the demands of his ideal come into his deliberations concerning what he may or must do, the demands are not those of prudence. Yet at the same time they are self-regarding; for they refer to his own personal ideal of moral development. It matters for him what the significance, for that development, would be of the alternative actions before him. Self-regarding considerations may therefore, in referring to one's ideal, be nonprudential, nonselfish, and at the same time eminently moral.

Of course, ideal considerations can easily slip into prudential ones. If Gandhi's system of values had changed in later life to one in which the *sole* value was the spiritual one, the vision of God, then the attainment of ideal qualities of character might have insensibly become a merely prudential objective, supposing that the attainment was considered useful in the achievement of the vision. There is often an ambiguity in this respect. The Stoic can easily slip into Epicureanism. The 'good Christian' may turn out to be just another extraordinarily prudent person. But it should be pointed out that if ideal ethics is likely to slide into prudence, the quasi-legal ethics of rules, rights, obligations, and duties suffers the same defect. It can easily happen that a person comes to abide by his obligations, not because that is what they are, but because he thinks there is something to gain by doing so. This tendency of ideal-oriented and obligation-oriented action to become prudential is not very surprising. What would a world be like in which the counsels of morality were continually at odds with the counsels of prudence? If many moral philosophers have tried mightily to reconcile the demands of morality and prudence, this is because they believe that when the voice of morality is inaudible, prudence can more easily be heard.

I want now to turn to a bothersome source of uncomfortableness with the notion that tacit or explicit references to
one's personal ideals can count as moral considerations. The
notion is that, unlike 'genuinely moral' considerations,
which rest on obligations and duties that are just there
whether we like it or not, considerations having to do with
our personal ideals do not have the same Gibraltar-like
quality. Personal ideals can be changed by personal decision.
They can, the critic might say, be conjured away by the
arbitrary decision of the individual himself, who is faced
with the requirements of the ideal in practice. So, none of
the requirements of the ideal are quite solid. They are always
subject to the ideal's not being changed by decision of the
person whose ideal it is. What is at issue is whether, *because I
can change* my ideals, appeals to them do not count as moral
considerations, since moral considerations refer to what is
beyond my power to change.

But this is, so far, an obtuse kind of criticism. It is not
change per se, it is reasoned change, that ought to be at
issue. We can, for good reason, come to have different ideas
concerning not only what our ideals should be but also what
our obligations and duties are. If ideals may change, so may
obligations; but we must not confuse whimsical, or, at any
rate, unreasoned, change, with changes that are made for
good reasons. A person may be a war advocate today and a
pacifist next week; everything depends on what has hap-
pened in his mind and heart in the interim. It surely does not
follow that merely because change in his ideals is possible,
those ideals must not be taken seriously in his decisions
about what to do. To deny this would be to ignore the
distinction that we know quite well how to make between
the person who lacks moral integrity and the person who,
through whatever changes he may pass, does not change
erratically, but changes for good reason, and who is firm in
his commitments. Even though Gandhi thought relatively
little of it in his earlier years, his thought toward the end of
his life began to be dominated by the desire to achieve
salvation, through the vision of God. It is therefore hardly
surprising that he became more and more interested in
achieving the self-purification that he believed to be the
prerequisite for such salvation and that his ideals of self-

purification, although always present in his pantheon of values, gradually shifted to a much higher position.

The critic may also have the idea that so long as ideals are 'purely personal', they are at least potentially fanatical or dangerous. There must be limits. It is morally wrong to set oneself an ideal that demands or condones the systematic torture of other human beings or bullying them into submission. And if a person brings into moral discussion considerations that refer to those ideals, then these are not, so the critic will insist, moral considerations. Personal ideals must always be open to criticism on moral grounds—always liable to rejection as being immoral. Therefore, the critic will insist, moral considerations may be distinguished from considerations that have to do with personal ideals, and they should be recognized as having priority in case of conflict.

The critic's wariness of appeals to personal ideals in moral discussion is easily understandable. Of course, we cannot accept as moral just any ideal that a person may adopt for himself. From the mere fact that he has certain ideals nothing whatever follows about the morality of the behavior that appeal to those ideals is intended to justify. For the ideals may themselves be rejected on moral grounds; and it hardly needs illustration that many ideals should be morally rejected. But the critic's argument is again an unfair one. He sets up a comparison between 'true' obligations and duties (those we know to be such) and personal ideals that we do *not* know to be morally defensible. Then he points to the moral danger of accepting references to these possibly immoral ideals in moral discussion. If he had recognized that we can be as mistaken in supposing that a claimed obligation is such as we can be in supposing that a personal ideal is morally defensible, then his argument would disappear.

It does not follow that because an ideal is personal, it is immune to moral criticism. But neither does it follow that because a personal ideal *can* be morally criticized, it should not be taken into account in making one's decisions. Even if, from some timeless point of view, there is the chance that an ideal may have to be abandoned as not being consistent with morality, it does not follow that from the point of view of the agent or observer at some point in time, the ideal does not entail requirements for action. To criticize an ideal as immoral is not to bring against it the possibility that it may not be able to meet future criticisms, but is to bring particular criticisms against it now.

A final point to notice is that obligations and duties are in one sense no less alterable by ourselves than are our ideals. For by agreement or consent we can create entitlements in other persons, enable the action of others, or waive our rights. By agreeing or consenting or waiving, we shift the moral landscape, creating new regions of obligations and duties and abolishing others. But it does not follow that because we can shift our duties and obligations about in this way, the resultant pattern of obligation and duty is therefore less binding.

Those theorists and ordinary folk who talk about 'morality' and about 'moral considerations' may have in mind different things. They may speak from different points of view or, one might even say, from different moral *Weltanschauungen*. A great deal of theoretical ethics may be understood as the attempt to reconcile these *Weltanschauungen* in ways that make sense. If a person is fixed on the picture of a *contractual* world in which everything turns on who has made what agreements, with whom, and to what effect, then moral considerations will for him all turn on 'underlying' or 'fundamental' tacit agreements on which all other agreements 'rest'. The only 'truly moral' considerations will have to do with what is owed to others according to previous understandings and with the current state of the moral balance sheet. It is from within this *Weltanschauung* that Hobbes and Locke, in different ways, viewed moral life and moral problems. Morality reduces to the keeping of agreements made; its analogue is contract law; all else is irrelevant.

Or a person may think of all 'truly moral' relations as those in which one person feels sympathy for or benevolence toward another; someone else may think of morality as consisting in obedience to 'moral law', a kind of super criminal law; for a third person, morality is seen in the common endeavor toward a community good. I have been defending the right of yet another sort of consideration to be taken into account: the sort that has to do with one's personal ideals of development. I have not argued that other moral points of view be excluded from moral deliberation or discourse or from normative ethics. I do not think of them as mutually exclusive. But I do hold that it is indefensible to assert or imply that considerations having to do with one's character ideals are irrelevant to moral decision, because the self-referential aspect of moral deliberation is the inevitable counterpart of the other aspects. We cannot speak only of agreements honored, sympathy exhibited, moral rules obeyed; we must also speak of persons' striving (or failing to strive) to be better, or anyway not worse, and of the relationship of this striving to the decisions that they make.

A full view of the problems of ethics inevitably extends our horizon from acts and problems to lives. We should not ask merely what the situation is that gives rise to the problem; we should also take into account the moral direction of lives. There are matters of moral biography and autobiography that cannot be ignored. The individual may want to know what he is making of his life, what he is becoming, what style of life he has fallen into, whether he is moving in the direction of some ideal. These questions about moral life do not have to do with honors awarded or merit accumulated; they have to do with what warrants the honors and with the credit balance of merit. They do not have to do with acts alone; they also have to do with the tendencies, attitudes, and dispositions of which the acts may be indicative. They do not have to do with achievements—battles won or fortunes made—although achievements of another sort may count, such as temptations resisted, friends made (or rejected), persons cared for. These latter achievements, however, are typically not goal directed in the way the former are. They are not the obtaining or reaching of something or some state. They are *attainments*. They tell us something about our progress or the lack of it.

It could be argued that moral worth is only to be found in the person who is to some degree conscious of his failings and vices, his virtues and triumphs, who examines his motives, questions his intentions, praises and blames himself, and urges himself on. In the process of self-formation he may keep ideals and models before him. Indeed, it is

difficult to understand how a person who was quite unconcerned about his moral standing and progress could at the
same time be amenable to moral considerations. How could
moral considerations have any leverage on such a being? But
these are not questions we can take up here. It will be
enough if we have identified and explored some of the
suspicions concerning the role of ideals in moral decision
and have allayed one or two of them.

PART 3

Education for Good Character

Among other pleasing errours of young minds, is the opinion of their own importance. He that has not yet remarked how little attention his contemporaries can spare from their own affairs, conceives all eyes turned upon himself, and imagines every one that approaches him to be an enemy or a follower, an admirer or a spy. He therefore considers his fame as involved in the event of every action. Many of the virtues and vices of youth proceed from this quick sense of reputation.
—Samuel Johnson, *The Rambler*, no. 196

Few that wander in the wrong way mistake it for the right; they only find it more smooth and flowery, and indulge their own choice rather than approve it; therefore, few are persuaded to quit it by admonition or reproof, since it impresses no new conviction, nor confers any powers of action or resistance.
—Samuel Johnson, *The Rambler*, no. 155

Sir, I love the acquaintance of young people; because, in the first place, young acquaintances must last longest, if they do last; and then, Sir, young men have more virtue than old men; they have more generous sentiments in every respect. I love the young dogs of this age: they have more wit and knowledge of life than we had; but then the dogs are not so good scholars.
—James Boswell, *The Life of Samuel Johnson*

8

On Avoiding Moral Indoctrination

> Morality in his sleep! Place the Moraltutor (patented)
> under your child's pillow, tuck him in, and set him on the
> road to rectitude. Operates at a cost of less than 2¢ per
> day. Designed by noted psychologists and engineers;
> approved by leading public figures; widely used in public
> institutions. Just clip the form below. . . .

The implications for moral education of my argument
against reductivism in ethical theory, and for a virtue-
oriented approach to ethics, remain to be made out. I will
hold that the primary aim of moral education is to encourage
the development of the right sort of person. Before we can
approach the questions of what the right sort is and how to
persuade it to come into being, we must make some distinctions. We must distinguish between moral training and
moral indoctrination; we must also distinguish between
defensible and indefensible indoctrination. That is the task
of this chapter.

Philosophers and ordinary men, or some of them anyway, shudder at the notion of moral indoctrination. It is not
clear what is the object of this reaction, nor why shuddering
is more appropriate than cheering. In a recent debate, three
suggestions have been made for what indoctrination consists
in: method, content, and aim. In this chapter, I want to
examine these suggestions and to offer some distinctions,
which I hope may advance the discussion.

I am particularly grateful for the comments of Kurt Baier and also for those of
William Frankena, R. S. Peters, and Israel Sheffler. This chapter was published as
chapter 4 in *Educational Judgments*, ed. James Doyle (Routledge & Kegan Paul, 1973).

I will begin with remarks made by John Wilson and R. M. Hare.[1] Wilson starts out by rejecting the suggestion that to indoctrinate is to employ any particular method of instruction. That 'indoctrinate' cannot be defined in this way is, he thinks, apparent from the fact that whereas the employment of certain methods, such as hypnotism, would be regarded as indoctrinating if they were used to inculcate religious, political, or moral beliefs, the same methods, when employed for the teaching of Latin grammar or the multiplication tables, would not count as indoctrination. According to Wilson's way of looking at the matter, a 'Mathtutor' would not be an indoctrinating device, whereas a 'Moraltutor' would be, even if the devices were electronically identical.

If, however, indoctrination does not consist in the employment of any particular method, it must have to do, Wilson holds, with the content of instruction. Indoctrination consists in teaching what is uncertain as if it were certain. Beliefs are uncertain if "it is not true that any sane and sensible person, when presented with the relevant facts and arguments, would necessarily hold the beliefs. We might put this by saying that there was no *publicly-acceptable* evidence for them, evidence which any rational person would regard as sufficient" (pp. 27–28). Education, on the other hand, consists in instructing in such a way that the certainty with which a doctrine is taught is directly related to the publicly acceptable evidence available for its support. Moral beliefs are uncertain, not merely in the sense that there is not enough such evidence for their support, but also in that we are not sure what kind of evidence it takes to support them. "We cannot even be sure that any question of truth, falsehood, or evidence arises at all with metaphysical and moral issues . . . we do not know exactly how they are important. We do not know how to tackle them" (p. 30). Yet moral beliefs, even if not completely certain, may be taught in such a way that only that degree of certainty is claimed for them which is warranted by the public evidence available for their support. There will, then, be beliefs and behavior which every sane and sensible person believes should be taught because enough evidence is available to warrant our teaching them. I do not understand how Wilson can qualify as sane and sensible those people who (1) do not know whether there can be evidence for moral beliefs and (2) hold that there is sufficient evidence for a moral belief to teach it to our children. At any rate, he holds that what warrants our labeling the teaching as indoctrination is not so much a matter of how morality is taught, by what devices or methods, as of the uncertain nature of the subject matter that is taught as certain.

Hare thinks that Wilson's way of analyzing indoctrination will not do, since it would allow indoctrinators to pose as educators. ''For who are to count as sane and sensible people? Most people think that they themselves and the majority of their friends are sane and sensible people. So if that is what Mr. Wilson says, he will not succeed in barring the way to a great many educational practices that I am sure he would want to call indoctrination'' (Hare, p. 48). Once we admit Catholics, Communists, Anglicans, and other potential indoctrinators into the fold as sane and sensible, then we have no ground on which to reject their claim that the beliefs they teach are certain, since the criterion of certainty in a belief is that sane and sensible people, when presented with the relevant facts and arguments, necessarily hold it. Hence, we have no ground for rejecting the inculcation of religious or moral catechisms, by whatever means, as indoctrination.

In place of method or content, Hare would put aim. Aim is what enables us to distinguish the indoctrinator from the educator. ''Indoctrination only begins when we are trying to stop the growth in our children of the capacity to think for themselves about moral questions. If all the time that we are influencing them, we are saying to ourselves, 'perhaps in the end they will decide that the best way to live is quite different from what I am teaching them; and they will have a perfect right to decide that,' then we are not to be accused of indoctrinating'' (p. 52). The aim, on Hare's view, will influence the method of moral education, and this in turn will influence the content. Given the aim of keeping the child's mind open on moral matters, we will not use methods that will shut off teacher and pupil from ''the fresh winds of argument.'' The aim of the educator is to get the pupil to think for himself, so his method is to discuss moral questions with him ''with no holds barred and no questions banned, and is himself prepared to ask the questions again—

really ask them—and is prepared to answer them in a different way from the way he has up till now, if that is the way the argument goes" (p. 53).

The form of moral education which flows from its aim has to do, as readers of Hare's moral philosophy might suspect, with prescriptivity and universalizability. "What we have to teach people, if we are educating them morally, is to ask themselves the question 'What kind of behavior am I ready to prescribe for myself, given that in prescribing it for myself, I am prescribing it also for anybody in a like situation?'" (p. 61). Pupils must be educated in such a way that in later life they will be free to adopt different principles from the ones we have taught them, provided the new principles are prescriptive and universalizable too. "At the end of it all, the educator will insensibly stop being an educator, and find that he is talking to an equal, to an educated man like himself—a man who may disagree with everything he has ever said; and, unlike the indoctrinator, he will be pleased" (p. 70).

Indoctrination need not be a bad thing. To say that a person has been indoctrinated is, according to *Oxford English Dictionary*, to say that he has been "imbued with a doctrine, idea, or opinion." Indoctrination, if this definition be accepted, need not be a bad thing; because it is sometimes morally justifiable to become imbued with a doctrine. Peace Corps volunteers, new teachers in an experimental school, or workers for a political party may expect to undergo indoctrination. That is, they may not only learn the full implications of the commitment they have made, but they may also try to absorb the doctrine, to make it a part of themselves, so that they do not have to wonder or worry about what to say or do in situations that are apt to arise. To this end, they may with clear consciences attend classes, feign debates, and memorize passages of the relevant literature. They may even, when they feel that they are getting rusty on matters of doctrine, attend reindoctrination classes so that they will get a fresh grasp on doctrinal matters that bear on the problems that arise in the lives that they have set for themselves. The question, then, is not When does education become indoctrination? as if indoctrination were necessarily a bad thing, but When does education become indefensible indoctrination? or When does education indefensibly become indoctrination?

To say that education becomes indefensible indoctrination is to say that it becomes a form of brainwashing. 'Brainwashing' may be used as the generic term for techniques of indoctrination (involving torture, electronic devices, or what have you) that make it psychologically impossible for a person to deliberate to any purpose about certain matters. In the present context, the deliberation in question would be about what one ought, morally speaking, to do. The brainwashed person would typically be imbued with the belief that there is some authority (the Pope, the King, the Book) that will infallibly tell him what is right and that there is nothing to do but to obey. Or he might be brainwashed into accepting some more abstract principle as the universal determinant of right action, such as that whatever promotes eternal salvation or is in accordance with natural law or forwards the cause of communism is right.

To say that education indefensibly becomes indoctrination is to say that the pupil is indoctrinated under the pretense that he is being educated. He has not deliberated about and then chosen certain doctrines in which he then wishes to become indoctrinated; he is indoctrinated willy-nilly. He is indoctrinated unawares, by means that would be permissible had he freely and justifiably chosen to be indoctrinated. Sometimes the term 'orientation' is used to refer to this normally inoffensive form of indoctrination. 'Orientation' presupposes the will of the student to entrust to the indoctrinator the task of helping the student to find his bearings. But the trust is revocable and is understood as such by both student and teacher. The indefensibility of indoctrination arises here from the lack of any such tacit or explicit understanding, from the student's being indoctrinated by means that insensibly confirm him in beliefs that he has not freely chosen, from his being led toward an irrevocable trust in the landmarks with which the indoctrination supplies him. An example of education's indefensibly becoming indoctrination might be the kind of instruction in military techniques which takes the volunteer all unawares into a

kind of political indoctrination in which he is imbued with
the belief that there are no legitimate grounds upon which
the command of a military superior may be questioned.
Whether it is brainwashing or orientation in, and thus
confirmation in, a belief not freely chosen, the consequence
is that the right to think for oneself has been surrendered or
taken away.

What is it about *moral* beliefs that gives the child the right
(eventually) to make up his own mind about them? I
do not find a very satisfactory answer either in Wilson's or in
Hare's account. Wilson's notion, as we have seen, is that
these beliefs tend to be uncertain and that if we don't honor
the child's right to question them, we are treating what is
uncertain as if it were certain. Therefore we may drum in the
multiplication tables in a way in which we have no right to
drum in moral beliefs. But even if it is certain that five times
five is twenty-five, why should we try to prevent a child
from questioning it? It is not clear that we should drum in
anything in this mindless way; hence it is not clear that
different methods are appropriate to certain and uncertain
subject matter. And as Hare argues, the criterion of certainty
becomes crucial on such an account. If it is that a certain class
of people, self-nominated as sane and sensible, believes the
doctrine for reasons they regard as true and relevant, then
Wilson's definition has failed to catch indoctrinators in its
net. Therefore, in criticizing Wilson's account, we need not,
fortunately, take up the question of whether there are any
moral beliefs that are certain or of what, exactly, Wilson
means when he says that there are none.[2]

Against Hare's insistence that indoctrination consists in
teaching a child in such a way that he is not free to think for
himself, I would insist that not all indoctrination is of this
sort; only bad indoctrination is. I would agree, however, that
all moral indoctrination is bad. The question then is, What
grounds do we have for presuming that children have a
right, when they become adults, to be able to make up their
own minds on matters of moral belief? It is to this subject
that we now turn.

Hare's answer can be put roughly by saying that children have a right to make up their own minds concerning moral beliefs because they will need to be able to do so in the circumstances in which they will live.[3] These circumstances are likely to be sufficiently different from those in which their parents and teachers live that the beliefs (principles) that the adults live by will not suffice when the child becomes an adult. The child must therefore be free to adapt himself to the world in which he must live. Moral indoctrination would be bad on this account, because it would interfere with the child's right to adjust his moral views to the changing world in which he must live. In *The Language of Morals,* Hare makes use of the analogy of teaching a person to drive. Since you can't always be telling him exactly what to do next, you must try to give him some general principles to follow, which he will learn to make use of only gradually, by applying them to very many different kinds of situations. In the moral life, we must not only flesh out the principles we are taught but even, on occasion, abandon them altogether, or adopt new ones.

The right not to be indoctrinated may be said, then, on Hare's account, to rest on the right to adapt oneself to change: call it the right of adaptation. In a way this is a perfectly satisfactory account. Indeed, as a parent, I cannot possibly claim to foresee every situation that my child will have to face in his life. Truth is stranger than prediction. It would be a sin against him if I were to teach him in such a way that he could not figure out for himself what to do, but felt bound by beliefs that I have given to him or was immobilized by my ghostly and inappropriate admonitions. I will, then, give him something procedural. I will not teach him in such a way that he will have to use my principles forever, but I will tell him how, when the time comes, he can find principles of his own. This he will be able to do if I teach him the place that logic, facts, imagination, and inclination should have in his thinking.[4] But when I think about Hare's account a second time, I find that I am not so clear.

The right of adaptation rests upon a supposed need— the need to adapt. But what kind of need is this? In Hare's analogy, we can see the point. Hare does not, I think, have so much in mind that cars or traffic rules will change as that new situations will arise, which will require a change in driving tactics. (Hare might have distinguished these possibilities, since the choice of one interpretation over the others bears on the account that one might naturally give of Hare's key term, 'principle'.) The need of the student, in any case, is to *cope with new problems*. These problems are such, because if he does not cope successfully, he will have collisions. But what, in moral education, corresponds to collisions? The student needs to adapt to new situations, meaning that he must learn to solve new problems, because if he does not do so, he will . . . what? What is the danger or unhappy consequence which the student must avoid? I do not wish to deny that there is a need to adapt to changing circumstances, to shrug off the dead hand of the past; but how does this apply to the moral life? The only thing to say that sounds plausible is that the student must avoid immorality: he must be moral. He must cope with new problems in such a way that he will not jeopardize his claim to being a moral person. And a moral person is . . . ? How am I to avoid a circle? If I say that he is a person who lives by certain principles, then I am begging the question. For the question is why a person may need to change his principles, any of his principles. But if I say that he is a person who adapts his principles to the situation in which he lives, then I am saying that a student must not be indoctrinated, because he has a right of adaptation. Why? Because he must be the kind of person who can adapt. We must begin again.

When Hare says that the aim of education, lest it become indoctrination, must not be to stop the growth of the capacity of a child to think for himself about moral questions, what does he have in mind as a moral question? The examples he gives (pp. 52–53) are of widely different sorts. He mentions the questions of the ''best way to live,'' that is, as a Catholic, a Communist, or a bearer of the American way of life. He mentions the question of whether one should lie, and the problems of sex and pacificism. These curt references must be considered against the background of *The Language of Morals* and *Freedom and Reason*, where, for example, he distinguishes between decisions of principle which presuppose a way of life, and decisions regarding which way of life to follow.[5]

Communism, Catholicism, and the American way of life are large and amorphous sets of beliefs; it is not at all difficult to imagine the pupil's coming to reject any of them, for reasons that he would gladly give to his tutor. It is easy also to imagine his having a debate with his tutor and his rejecting his tutor's views, when the question is whether trial marriages are morally defensible or whether there can ever be a war in which a man can participate with a clear conscience. He might also come to a more liberal interpretation of lying, so that the tutor's rigorism is tempered by qualifications that the tutor would not have admitted. But how far can this ultimate disagreement, this thinking for oneself on moral matters, go? What does and does not count as a moral belief when Hare asserts that the pupil must be free to think for himself? Is it a belief, which the pupil may return, as an adult, to debate with his tutor—for example, that he should be honest (straightforward, nondevious), humane (sympathetic, not cruel), or just (fair, equitable, even-handed)?

When we speak of beliefs, and even more when we speak of principles, the picture we have is likely to be that of people taking positions in a debate. If it is a belief, then it must be open to challenge. A principle must be a place where we can begin in an argument. When Hare says that the pupil must come to be a "man who may disagree with everything [his teacher] says," we want to ask whether he can by the same token reject everything the teacher is—not just his beliefs and principles but also the traits of character that are evident in his life.

If the teacher teaches that what is dishonest is wrong, he must do so out of his life: if he is to succeed as a teacher of morality, he must show himself (not exhibit himself) to be an honest man. It is not something he says, not a principle he adopts, not a doctrine he promulgates. When he exhibits his repulsion at a cruel act or when he punishes his pupil for torturing a cat, he is not ipso facto taking a position.

I suspect that Hare and Wilson presuppose a certain background of moral education that 'everyone' has: an education in which qualities of character such as honesty and courage are inculcated early. It is only against this background that the appearance of extreme relativism can arise, that disputes between teacher and erstwhile pupil are even possible. How can we suppose that the old pupil will come to his teacher's house to argue the 'belief' that one should be honest—not honest in this or that situation, but honest in general? Is he trying to persuade his teacher to be dishonest? If the former student is dishonest, there can be no assurance that he will debate fairly, that he will not misrepresent his own views and his teacher's views, that he will not distort the evidence, and that he will not make *ad hominem* sallies that he should not make. Dishonesty, if it were a subject for debate, which I deny, is at least not so in the way that Catholicism or communism or trial marriages are.

We might say that only people who have a certain character are free to disagree upon, to debate, matters of doctrine. For debate, there must be a certain degree of respect and trust. There must also be some agreement on what would count for or against a position. If Wilson is right that we do not know how to 'do' morals, then we do not know how to carry on a moral discussion. It might be said, on the other hand, that the presupposed agreement in carrying on a moral debate need not be moral agreement, since without that we can agree to reject positions that can be shown to be inconsistent. Indeed, anyone who is able to recognize and point out an inconsistency is able to show that a 'position' is not a position.

But not everyone is eligible to discuss moral issues. As Hare may recognize, but does not emphasize, only the person who can be affected by moral reasons or is amenable to moral reasons is eligible. Among other things, this means that he must be able to entertain counter examples. He must be the sort of person who can recognize that if a doctrine entails that he must do a certain thing, then it must be wrong, since he could never do such a thing—because to do so would be dishonest or cruel, say. If it were open—a matter of discussion—whether to be dishonest, then a whole range of counter examples could have no effect on him, and consequently he would not be qualified to debate matters of doctrine from the moral point of view.

What would a debate be like over the question of whether dishonesty is a bad thing? What sorts of considerations would count for or against the thesis? Would it be said, for example, that dishonesty aids self-expression and that whatever aids self-expression is right? But then, how are we to know what counter examples would be acceptable against the self-expression theory of moral rightness, if examples of the dishonesty that it could entail would not count? Would it be said that the 'policy' that one should be as dishonest as possible could not become a universal prescription? How are we to know, if everything is up for grabs, that this will count either? If there are no requirements regarding what qualities of character he should have, why should the debater not argue that we live in a dishonest world and that we should be realists, giving and taking our lumps as the occasion makes possible or demands?

It is hard to imagine what a debate would be like on the 'doctrine' that dishonesty is a bad thing. It would amount, I suppose, to a discussion of the question of whether and why one should be moral. And it is certainly the case that intellectually curious people will want to raise and discuss that question. It is a peculiar issue, in that it can't be kept at arm's length; it inevitably takes an *ad hominem* turn. I suspect that this is because it is not clear who is supposed to be discussing the matter. If he is a person for whom 'that would be dishonest' counts as a reason against doing an action, then he is in that respect moral, and the argument is pleonastic. If he is not, then how is it to be settled? By appeal to his self-interest? But how is it going to make a man amenable to moral counter example to show him that it is in his self-interest to be so? This is a matter of character, not of beliefs or principles; of what he is, not of what he holds.

It might even be said that it is precisely in his being amenable to counter examples that show the dishonesty of a course of action that a man is free to debate the issue of whether a principle or a belief that would require that course of action should be accepted. If he does not know what would count pro or con in such a discussion, whether he is ahead or behind, whether he has won or lost, then he can only be free to enter the discussion in a Pickwickian kind of way. He is free to engage in it in the way that a child is free to 'play' chess by shoving the pieces around on the board.

S o far, I have agreed with Hare that to say that A is a
moral indoctrinator is to say that he has a certain aim:
namely, to prevent the child from thinking for himself. I
have raised the question of what kind of thing the pupil may
think for himself about, and I have expressed reservations
about the kind of rationale that Hare might give for the thesis
that the child must not be prevented from thinking for
himself. That thesis, which I hope I have not unfairly
attributed to Hare but which is interesting in its own right
anyway, is that because the child must adjust to the unpredictable world, he has the right not to be educated in such a
way as to make this adjustment impossible. I want to return
to this matter now, with another kind of account, which
Hare might accept too, of the wrongness of moral indoctrination.

The demand that each person should be free to think for
himself is the consequence of his responsibility for the moral
beliefs that he holds. When he becomes an adult, he will be
held answerable for his wrongdoing. He cannot avoid this
responsibility by saying that he did what he did because his
parents or his teacher told him to do it; nor can he appeal to
the command of a dictator, the canons of his church, or the
laws of the state. If parent, teacher, dictator, church, or state
provides him with general principles that he must follow in
making decisions, then if he invokes these principles in
justification of his action, they become his principles; and he
is responsible for them, too. By accepting them, he signals
acceptance of himself as the kind of person who is governed
by those principles. If they are attacked, he must defend
them. He could have chosen other principles, but he has not
done so.

It is as if, in preparing for battle, he has a choice of the
weapons he will carry into the fray. He will then not be able
to blame the outcome on his weapons. He cannot excuse
himself by saying "If only I had chosen a sword instead of a
dagger, I would surely have won," since it was open to him
to have chosen a sword. The excuse is even less successful if
he is free to exchange weapons as the nature of the battle
changes. Here the analogy with moral education can be
made closer, if we imagine that the first distribution is made
by a tutor who tries to foresee what the exigencies of the

battle will require but who realizes his limitations as a prophet and therefore makes it possible for the pupil to exchange weapons as the battle progresses. The point is not just that the pupil must adjust but also that he is responsible for what he makes of himself. It is he, not his teacher, who will be approved or disapproved, punished or rewarded, canonized or anathemized. This ultimate responsibility—not just for his actions but also for being the kind of person that he is as revealed by the kind of reasons (principles) he cites in justification of his actions—is what makes it morally mandatory that the pupil should be educated in such a way that he can think for himself. He wants to become an adult for the very good reason that he will be treated as an adult; to shove him into the world an eternal child is morally unjustifiable.

A principle can, on Hare's view, be something that can be discovered by observing a person's behavior or something that is offered in justification of his behavior, but the distinction is too important to risk losing under a common term.[6] (It might be helpful to refer to a principle in the first sense as a character trait and to use the generic term 'moral belief' for [nonfactual] reasons why an action is held to be right.) The important point, for moral education, is that even if we worry with and about our moral characters all of our lives, they tend to be formed early. The teacher, then, must be actively interested in how they are formed. He must encourage the development of some character traits and discourage the development of others. To raise the question of whether, in pursuit of these objectives, he is engaged in moral indoctrination is confusing. If he is not inculcating moral beliefs, then he is not doing so in an indefensible way. The individual who has had a good moral education will not only give and be guided by the right reasons, he will have the right instincts, the right reactions. This is a result, not of indoctrination, but of training. There can be bad training as well as bad indoctrination. Fagin's training of Oliver Twist was bad, not because he aimed to make it impossible for Oliver to think for himself, but because he made him into a thief and an artful dodger. That Oliver would not be likely, as a result of his training, to bother his head about moral matters was incidental. Fagin was notorious, not for the doctrines he taught, but for forming his boys' characters in the way that he did. To have been subjected to bad training is to have the wrong reactions; to have been the victim of bad indoctrination is to have a closed mind where minds should be open.

To return to the reason of why moral indoctrination is bad: it is so because it makes the pupil liable to be held answerable for what should be, but is not, his own thinking. He is held answerable, not in the external way in which the criminal law holds a person answerable for the violation of a law that he had no way of knowing existed, but for a blameworthy fault—the failure to live by morally defensible beliefs. If he has been brainwashed, he has an acceptable excuse; but if indoctrination merely inhibits his capacity to think for himself, he has not. The point is that he cites his moral beliefs as reasons for acts that he does, but if the belief really requires the action and if the action is morally wrong, then something is morally amiss with the person who lives by that belief, and it will not suffice as an excuse that he was taught to believe as he does.

Aristotle remarked that "by choosing what is good or bad we are men of a certain character, which we are not by holding certain opinions."[7] This is either true or false, depending on how we interpret 'opinions'. If 'opinions' are the beliefs we hold on doctrines over which moral persons can disagree, such as the question as to whether participation in a war can ever be justified or whether trial marriages can ever be a permissible practice, then what Aristotle says is true. Moral persons must be free to debate such issues. No position can be ruled out in advance as a position that is not open to a moral person. Indoctrination is a way of closing off debatable issues from debate, by making a person believe that to take the 'wrong' position is ipso facto to be immoral. We cannot, however, rightly accuse a person of dishonesty, cruelty, injustice, or lack of integrity *merely* in virtue of his holding that trial marriages are morally justifiable. What we can do is attempt to show him that his position pro or con would entail his making choices that would require him to be dishonest, cruel, and so forth. He may or may not admit this. But if he does freely choose to do a dishonest thing, on the basis of any doctrine or belief whatever, then he is, in that respect, a 'man of a certain character': he is dishonest. Moreover, if his beliefs are his justification for being dishonest, then he is blameable for holding a belief that, as he believes, justifies his being dishonest. For no belief can do this; and he cannot avoid blame by appeal to one. He is in this sense responsible for his beliefs, in that if he 'chooses what is bad' as a consequence of them, he must either reject them or admit that they truly represent him, characterize him.

If, on the other hand (Aristotle surely did not mean this) 'opinions' are to the effect that what is dishonest, cruel, or unjust should not be done, then Aristotle's remark would be false, or, rather, it would be unintelligible. For an 'opinion' is something which, in the context, can be put forward for moral debate, something on which we can take a moral position. But there can be no moral debate of the question of whether dishonesty is a bad thing.

This is to say, not that it is a 'matter of definition' that dishonesty is bad, but that it is a matter of eligibility for moral discussion or for discussion from the moral point of view. I do not deny that someone can claim that dishonesty is a good thing, that life has more savor with a dash of dishonesty, that dishonesty helps self-expression, and so forth, and that therefore it should not be discouraged. I hold that if a person takes what he says seriously enough not to recognize that 'that is dishonest' is a count against his action, he is ineligible to discuss moral beliefs.

No one is a moral indoctrinator, then, because he inculcates in his pupil a distaste for dishonesty, a revulsion against cruelty, or a sense of outrage at injustice. In teaching his pupil in such a way as to encourage these *qualities of character*, he is not closing his pupil's mind, stunting his growth, or making it impossible for him to think for himself. He is, rather, giving him the *kind of character* without which he would be unable to carry on a moral discussion. To help a child to develop the qualities of character that I have mentioned is, in fact, to open up new possibilities for him of thinking for himself. For he cannot be said to have the traits in question unless he has learned to think in a certain way.

To become a person who is repelled by dishonesty, he must learn to recognize dishonesty when it occurs in others or in himself. This means that mindless training will not do. If he is to recognize cruelty, he cannot be trained simply to be repelled by the presence of suffering. This clearly will be insufficient if he is to have it as a trait of character that he is a humane person. It is not enough, even, that he be trained so as to be revolted by the infliction of suffering. Sometimes dentists and headmasters make others suffer for good reason, not because they are cruel. The pupil must be so trained (here 'educated' may be more appropriate) that he will be repelled by the taking of pleasure in the suffering of another. But this is not a simple response to a stimulus; understanding is required as an intermediary. Far from closing the mind, moral training provides it with the fundamental considerations against which moral beliefs may be tested. It makes it possible for the child to think for himself. With moral training and, consequently, with a developing moral character, he is able to evaluate the doctrines and principles, the beliefs, that are proposed to him. Without moral training, he cannot.

That the position I have outlined smacks of intuitionism I am uncomfortably aware. It is true that if to be an intuitionist is, at least, to claim that there is a particular kind of knowledge, my position is not intuitionist. For on my view, the person who rejects a course of action as dishonest is not making a knowledge claim. He is saying what he cannot do and, by implication, what he cannot be. But even if my position is not intuitionistic in the ordinary epistemological sense, it does say, in common with other intuitionistic positions, that there is an area that is not open to serious discussion—an area that is off bounds for a moral person.

As philosophers, we do not take kindly to the suggestion that there are matters that we may not seriously question; but we should understand the price that we pay in claiming the right to question. Seriously to maintain that it is an open question whether it is a count against an action that it would be cruel is to maintain that it is an open question whether moral beliefs that require such actions can be evaluated on the ground that they would require cruelty of us. Skepticism with respect to the relevance of charges of injustice and dishonesty remove more criteria of evaluation. But if all of the criteria by which we evaluate beliefs are themselves open to doubt, it is open to doubt whether evaluation is possible. We cannot, however, lapse at this point into a comfortable skeptical acquiescence. For if there were no way of evaluating moral beliefs, then it would make no sense to try to discuss them or to debate which of them we should choose. And if it makes no sense to debate, we cannot object to indoctrination on the ground that it un- justifiably teaches what is debatable as if it were what all right-minded people necessarily believe.

9

On Becoming the Right Sort

Moral education is at once the most complex and the simplest, the most frustrating and the most rewarding, the most challenging and the easiest, task of the teacher. It is complex because of the number of conceptions (and misconceptions) of its purpose and because of the number of means to achieve 'the' purpose that are in the field; it is simplest because there are straightforward and obvious things that the teacher can do to aid moral development. It is frustrating because the teacher is not, even in his own school, the only, or necessarily the most important, influence on the child's development of character; it is rewarding because nothing can seem more important than the revelation of admirable qualities in a child that are teacher inspired. It is challenging because the task is obviously centrally important and endlessly difficult; it is easy because the most effective procedure is to serve as a model of the sort of person the teacher would hope that the child should become.

In what follows, I will be mostly concerned with background questions—questions that should be taken up first before setting out too confidently on some kind of 'moral education program'. My title is the least question-begging way that I can think of to indicate my topic and my general approach.

What is it to be the right sort of person? Some very profound and some very silly things have been said on this subject; and it is not always easy to be sure on which side mysterious or unclear pronouncements fall. It has been said that the right sort of person should be autonomous, that he should be morally perfect, that he should have realized himself, that he should have fulfilled himself, that he should be free, that he should be the possessor of a certain kind of intuitive knowledge, that he should be socialized, that he should be fully developed, that he should be morally rational, that he should be a servant of God. These global and intimidating requirements are intended to sum up what is the end of moral learning. Each of them is intended to serve as a compendium of virtue and of vice.

Another kind of answer to the question of what it is to be the right sort of person is one that picks out a particular virtue as the compendium of virtue. One is the right sort if one is (really and fully) just or conscientious or benevolent. To be just, in the full sense, is to be courageous, loyal, honest, and so forth—to have all of the virtues. And so on for conscientiousness, benevolence, and so forth.[1]

Answers of this compendium sort have, I think, a disadvantage that overweighs their advantages. The advantages are that by thinking in this global way about what the end or purpose of 'moral education' is, a single target is set up, rather than multiple targets, and that a common understanding of the ends of 'moral education' is thereby made possible. The disadvantage is that compendium targets tend to be themselves poor guides for the seeker of the answer to the original question, What is it to be the right sort of person? The route from the global objective of the attainment of freedom, say, to some specification of the characteristics of the right sort of person is a perilously vague one. If the model of freedom is a Nietzschean one, then the set of characteristics will be very different from the set that will follow from having attained the sort of freedom that attracts a John Stuart Mill, and that model of freedom will generate different qualities than a Sartrean model would. In discussing which of these models is preferable, one inevitably comes back to the question of what qualities of character the model would approve or disapprove. There is good reason, then, to move directly to the question of what are the more specific qualities of character that are desirable.

Rather than begin with an enveloping carpetbag of an answer, it will be more useful to assemble first the items that

we would like any suitable carpetbag to contain. I now turn
to that task.

To say that Abel is the right sort of person is, as I will use
that expression, to say that Abel has qualities of character, virtues, that make him preferable to Baker, Charlie, or
anyone else who lacks those qualities of character. Qualities
of character are just those dispositions the possession of
which can be our ground for preferring one person to
another—preferring in general, that is. A special ground that
we may have for preferring Abel to Baker as a painter might
be that he does not drip paint on the shrubbery. It is a
general ground for preference that Abel is honest and that
Baker is not. Specificity and generality are relative matters;
but some qualities are such that it is difficult to imagine a
social order in which persons who have them are not
preferable to persons who do not have them.

What, then, are the most general dispositional grounds
for preferring one sort of person to another sort? The answer
to this question will tell us what sort of person is the right
sort. Before we take it up, one more field-narrowing move
can be made. Since we are here interested in learning to be
the right sort, we are interested only in those qualities that
are at least in part the result of some effort of learning on the
part of the person. This rules out 'native' dispositions,
whether acquired through the genes or in very early childhood, over which Abel has no control: intelligence, the
capacity to carry a tune, and sense of humor may serve as
examples.

In asserting that a given disposition provides general
grounds for preference, I will try to make explicit the
assumptions of fact about the world that makes it such that a
disposition of this sort is desirable. It is necessary to do this
so that one can see the reason for preferring that disposition
to its opposite. The assumptions of fact will be largely
noncontroversial ones, as we see. Taken together, these
assumptions constitute a thumbnail sketch of 'the human
situation', of the conditions, that is, under which human
beings 'must' (given the nature of the physical world and of
human nature and human association) live. The ethics that

results from taking these dispositions—the central virtues—
as the object of moral education is, in the above sense, a
'naturalistic' one: it says what human dispositions are and
are not desirable, not on the basis of some transcendent
deduction or of intuition, but, rather, on the desirability or
undesirability of those dispositions in 'the human situation'.[2]

The answer to the question of what characteristics the
right sort of person will have should, then, be a
relatively uncontroversial one. Assuming that nearly anything worth having will require a good deal of concerted
effort, then persistence, courage, and unflappability in the
face of setbacks will be universally desirable instrumental
virtues—instrumental, that is, to the attainment of anything
that is difficult to attain. Given that in the ordinary course of
things tempers will sometimes flare and that there will
sometimes be vehement disagreements on where to go or
how to proceed, the diplomatic virtues of tolerance and tact
will be valuable. Given that there must be common understandings concerning what is permitted and what is required, the tendency to take advantage of others by violating
the understandings, while they are by and large at the same
time being faithful to them, is a vice. Given that distributions
must sometimes be made according to merit or some other
agreed-upon criterion, then we will value nondiscrimina-
toriness, or fairness.

It would be tedious to go far with such a list; but the
point has, I think, already been made that we share a good
deal of well-grounded agreement on the question of who is
the right sort of person in general. If the choice is to be made
against the background of a particular task or position, we
may be able to find agreement on dispositional criteria there
too. It is often far easier to agree on the criteria to be met or
approached by a candidate for a position than to find a
candidate who clearly meets the requirements.

In thinking through what dispositions a child should be
helped to acquire, we must consider carefully the exigencies
of the life through which the child is to pass. Perhaps this is
why Aristotle, who thought of ethics as the study of what is

desirable and undesirable in character, contended (*EN*, 1095a) that ethics is a study for those who have considerable experience of life but not for callow youths. Reflection on the common life and its exigencies may yield conclusions about which virtues are especially to be encouraged and which vices are especially to be discouraged. Here again, a central core of virtues and vices may emerge.

Selfishness is a vice that is especially destructive of human relations; so is deceptiveness; so is unfairness. Callousness—insensitivity to the feelings and interests of others—is a failing that will carry with it failings of other sorts: for example, the gratuitous infliction of suffering and pain, indifference to injustice, and the inability to appreciate the point of rules of common civility.

What is implicit in this account is a conception of the role of the teacher as a person who is better attuned to the demands of the world than is the child and who cares enough for the child (and for the world) to help the child develop the appropriate dispositions. It is to this matter that we now turn.

Caring for the child can too easily be converted by theory into questionable educational practices. The difficulty is that if we start from the unexceptionable premise that the teacher should care for the child, in the sense that he should do what is best for the child, and if we add to that a debatable premise about what 'doing what is best for the child' amounts to, we may arrive at a morally questionable conclusion. We may say that really to care for the child is to see to it that he is given full opportunity to develop as nature intended. This may lead us, in a Rousseauan mood, to say that the teacher's chief obligation is to stay out of the way and let nature take its course. On the other hand, if we add to the premise about the teacher's obligation to care for the child the premise that this requires conditioning that will protect the child against a cruel world, we may move to a Stoic conclusion that the appropriate thing to do is to inure the child not only to hardship but even to the most ordinary feelings of tenderness for another human being. That can, after all, increase the child's vulnerability to sorrow and disappointment.

What caring for the child, on the present understanding, amounts to is bringing the child to appreciate as fully as possible that certain qualities are virtues and that others are vices. Caring for the child demands this of the teacher for a number of reasons. Prudentially, from the child's point of view, it behooves him to cultivate the virtues and to avoid the vices since, unless he does cultivate them, in everything that matters to him he will not be preferred to persons who do. Morally, from the teacher's point of view, he ought to encourage his pupils to cultivate virtues and to avoid vices, since he is the member of the community in whose hands the future of the community is, largely, entrusted. He would fail to meet that trust if he failed to inculcate virtue (for short). Morally, from the teacher's point of view, he owes it to the child to help him appreciate the demands of virtue, because the child cannot fare well in the world unless he does appreciate those demands. Morally, from the child's point of view, he should cultivate the virtues because if he does not, the community will be, by so much, worse off. The community sustains him in the enjoyment and pursuit of everything that he recognizes as worthwhile. He therefore has an obligation of loyalty to the community not to undermine it but to sustain it. To become the right sort of person is to become the sort of person that the community needs, must have, if it is to continue as a desirable association. 'Desirability' must be defined largely by considering what the community would be like in the presence of dishonesty, injustice, cruelty—the vices.

'Appreciation' (or perhaps 'understanding' or 'realization') is a better word here than 'knowledge'. It is not just the knowledge of which dispositions are virtues that the teacher must convey to the child.[3] Notoriously, 'cognition' is not enough; with the knowledge there must go the sense that what is known is important enough to act on, that it is not just another piece of information. For the child, it is a revelation of the way things are in the practical world, the world in which he is engaged as an actor, not merely as a spectator. He is an actor, not merely in the sense that he must cooperate—not be merely passive—in the acquisition of knowledge, but also in the sense that he is a participant in the activities about which he learns something when he learns about which dispositions are virtues and which are vices.

But what sort of 'moral education' enterprise, if any, is desirable in the public schools of a democratic state?[4] Is it enough for the teacher to help the child to appreciate what he should appreciate, given that the child is being initiated into a community that makes life tolerable for him or even desirable? Our comments so far are broad enough to cover the rationale for 'moral education' in a tribal village or in a national community governed by nondemocratic methods.

The apparent difficulty here is this: democratic government rests on certain doctrines; it is an ideology. To be good democrats, we must believe in freedom of thought and expression, free elections, representative government. The difficulty rests on the deeper notion that each person is a free agent, equally entitled to respect. A person may be virtuous, so it may seem, and fail to see the force of these doctrines. Do we really mean to contend that democratic doctrines have this characteristic—namely, that a truly virtuous person, no matter where, will be a proponent of democracy? That would be absurd. There have surely been thoroughly virtuous people who have held other than democratic views. We could start with Plato and go on.

Given this, must there then be a counterpart to virtue education or to helping the child to appreciate and eventually to attain virtue? Must there be indoctrination? But can indoctrination be justified at all, under any circumstances? Is not indoctrination at odds with the very notion of moral education, if moral education is an education that is to amount to more than conditioning to behave in appropriate ways? For does not moral education consist in part in the training to think critically, to use the head, in evaluating whatever doctrines are proposed to one?

A number of issues must (at the risk of repeating distinctions made in chapter 8) be sorted out here: (1) What is indoctrination? (2) Is indoctrination necessarily morally indefensible? (3) Need democratic values be imparted or inculcated by a process of indoctrination? (4) What is the distinction between indoctrination and moral training? What is wrong about indoctrination but right about moral training? (5) If democratic values are not imparted by indoctrination, then what assurance can there be that a 'moral-education program' will be supportive of democracy? (6) Does a good program of helping the child to appreciate virtues necessarily lead to his coming to appreciate democratic values? (7) Does the teaching of democratic values in a way that does assure the support of democracy, whether or not it is indoctrination, come into conflict with the task of helping the child to appreciate what are virtues and what are vices and thus of caring for the child who is entering the active world?

Let us approach these issues one by one. (1) What is indoctrination? For present purposes, it will do to say that it is teaching a doctrine in such a way (conditioning, drumming it in) that there is no opportunity for critical evaluation, for question, for finding out if the doctrine is right or wrong.

To ask whether indoctrination is necessarily morally indefensible (2) is to raise two different questions at once: (2a) Is indoctrination, as such, under any circumstances, morally indefensible? and (2b) Is indoctrination in morally defensible doctrines morally indefensible? The interest lies in the second question, because the sole hope of morally defending indoctrination lies in defending it as being necessary for the inculcation of morally defensible doctrines.

But what are the doctrines in question? They include the doctrine that thought and expression should be free. There is a kind of practical contradiction in drumming in a doctrine that is inconsistent with drumming in. The point of freedom of thought and expression is that people should be free to think for themselves, not to be told what to think. Does that not apply to the doctrine itself?—that it should be taught in a way that permits evaluation, critical questioning, rather than by indoctrination? So it would seem that it is morally indefensible, if it is not rationally incoherent, at the same time to proclaim a doctrine that drumming in is wrong, and then to drum that doctrine in.

(3) Need democratic values be imparted or inculcated by a process of indoctrination? and (4) What is the distinction between indoctrination and moral training? What is wrong about indoctrination but right about moral training? These questions belong together in that moral training may be

justified even though indoctrination is not. Indoctrination has to do with doctrines. When we speak vaguely of 'democratic values', we should be careful to distinguish those values that are doctrines from those that are not. A doctrine is, in principle, refutable, even though it may be strongly held for good and convincing reasons. It is a part of democratic doctrine that the state should allow as much freedom to the citizens as is consistent with the freedom and reasonable well-being of other citizens. This is a doctrine that has been and will be argued at length and criticized from a number of different points of view and against a variety of assumptions concerning the factual condition of the society for which this doctrine is being advocated. It is, on the other hand, not a part of democratic doctrine that cruelty or injustice are bad things. These are moral truisms that are not doctrines; they are not in principle refutable; they are the basis from which refutation (or approval) of any doctrine must begin. They may nevertheless be values—values for those persons who value democracy—but, of course, hardly the exclusive possession of advocates of democratic ideology.

Moral training, in the interest of helping the child to become the right sort of person, will bring the child both to recognize and to recognize the wrongness of cruelty and injustice. But the capacity to recognize the wrongness of these things is a necessary condition of understanding the moral force of a defense of a democratic (or any other) doctrine. It would be too much to claim that the child who has had the proper training will ipso facto embrace democratic doctrines. He will have to be shown the force of the moral arguments for those doctrines. He will be in a position to appreciate their force if he has had a good moral training.

If democratic values are not imparted by indoctrination, (5) what assurance can there be that a 'moral education program' will be supportive of democracy (of democratic doctrines)? To whatever extent the teacher is successful in encouraging the development of the right sort of person, he will produce the sort of person who can think to good effect about which doctrines are morally justifiable and which are not. That is as close to assurance that democratic doctrines will be supported by citizens who are the product of such a 'moral education' as we ought to want to come.

Our first loyalty in a moral-education program is to the good character of the child. A person of good character will have, among other things, good judgment. He will be able to think through the merits of political and other claims that he comes across. But at the same time he will know what commitment is. The capacity to make intelligent judgments and the capacity to be committed to democratic ideals will be at odds only if democratic ideals (or doctrines) fail to pass the test of critical evaluation. In that case, they will not be supported by the child who is the product of the moral-education process. But it is reasonable to assert that when the alternative doctrines are assessed, the morally well-educated child will come to approve of and to be committed to democratic doctrines.

(6) Does a good program of helping the child to appreciate the virtues necessarily lead to his coming to appreciate democratic values? I have already answered this question negatively. The only specifically democratic, as opposed to general moral, values are a set of doctrines having to do with principles governing the way in which political societies should be organized and administered. While it would be too much to say that the right sort of person will necessarily adopt these principles, there will, for him, be good reasons why he should. He will be well attuned to the claims of justice and of benevolence. Given, in addition, the sensitivity that he will have for the feelings and wants of others, a line of thought should easily suggest itself that will lead to the principle that given that one would like as much freedom as possible and that one can understand that others have a similar desire, it is only fair that as much freedom should be granted to each person as is consistent with the freedom of all. Additional thoughts about the necessity, in the interest of freedom and in the presence of large numbers of persons within the state, of representative government, may also suggest themselves. And so on. But then, to show that democratic principles ought to be congenial to the thought of the right sort of persons is not to show that they would necessarily be adopted or espoused by them.

(7) Does the teaching of democratic values in a way that does assure that the child will support democracy, whether or not the teaching amounts to indoctrination, come into conflict with the task of helping the child to appreciate what are virtues and what are vices, and thus caring for the child who is entering the active world? Caring for the child involves encouraging the development of moral judgment; but moral judgment cannot be neatly divided into judgment in private and in public affairs. Some of the same qualities of judgment—such as a sense of justice, concern for others, relevance to circumstances—are demanded both in private and in public affairs. If democracy will be supported by persons of good judgment, given certain assumptions of fact about background natural and social conditions (not everyone everywhere should be a citizen of a democracy), then it will be supported by persons who have been well cared for in that they have been helped to develop good judgment.

What does it mean to 'support' democracy, though? Surely it does not mean uncritical adulation, the mouthing of appropriate slogans. In the nature of the case, the democratic ideals must be argued for, and the force or the lack of force of the arguments must be appreciated. To argue to good effect is to understand the force of the counterarguments, of the opposing positions. To assure the support of democracy cannot mean that the appropriate slogans will be uttered and that individuals will receive emotional thrills at the mention of the word. It ought to mean the kind of critical approval that results from the application of moral (and generally practical) judgment to the question of what form of government is best and to the sense that there is an obligation to resist the development of any other form of government. (It is often said, justly, that democracy is not a perfect form of government, whatever that would be, but that in order to appreciate it, one must consider the alternatives.)

There is a more general issue that is raised by the question of whether moral education ought to be aimed at 'supporting' democracy. It is whether, supposing that the teacher's primary responsibility is to help the child become the right sort of person, there is anything that the child must come to accept or to reject in the way of moral conclusions of any sort. That is, beyond the question of political doctrines, are there specifically moral doctrines that the child must learn, on penalty of not being the right sort of person? It certainly seems as if there are moral truths that should become second nature to him: killing is wrong, lying is wrong, one's word should be kept, and so on. Could we possibly say of a person who disagreed with any of these conclusions that he was the right sort of person? Could we say, "He is the right sort, and believes that lying is O.K."? Probably not, given that it is understood that he is approving of lying in general, not just under special circumstances.

But why not? Well, lying is telling an untruth with the intent to deceive; but if he is the right sort, he will not be deceitful. He will have a 'natural' aversion to lying, cheating, or any other form of deception. The rest of the primitive moral injunctions in question—the 'moral rules'—seem to have similar relationships with being the right sort of person. If a person says that killing is all right—all right in general, not just under specially exonerating circumstances—then we have prima facie evidence that the person is deficient in his appreciation of the respect due to other persons. He is callous, cruel, or insensitive. He is not the right sort of person.

But if we move to less 'primitive' moral judgments, we are less inclined to tie being the right sort of person to holding the right opinions. Abel and Baker may both be of the right sort and still hold different opinions on the proper limits of individual freedom, on equal rights, or on penal justice. Abel may be generally liberal in his opinions; Baker may be generally conservative; at the same time they may both be of the right sort. It is in the nature of political doctrines that one is able simultaneously to respect and to disagree with the reasons that the opposition has for holding them—to think, for example, that one's own reasons are (far) weightier. To help a child to become the right sort is not to help him become a Republican or a Socialist but to help him think through the moral implications of the position that he does accept and to recognize its moral force and the force of opposing views.

The point applies equally to theological opinion. Indeed, there may be special qualities that are particularly valued within a Protestant or a Muslim community, but learning to be the right sort and doing what the teacher can to help that learning are not tied to any particular theological opinions. Whether moral learning is dependent on a belief in theological sanctions is another matter. It has seriously been questioned whether it is possible to have a meaningful moral-education program in the absence of and unconnected with religious instruction. It seems to me that it patently is possible.

Catholics can recognize that a Muslim is not just a good Muslim but that he is also the right sort of person; right-sortness can be recognized in Jews by Protestants, and so forth. Given this, it would seem that at least the steps of recognizing a moral model as such can be performed outside of religious boundaries. A just man is a just man is a just man. He needs no imprimatur to show forth what he is. Courage is no more a Catholic than it is a Buddhist virtue; honesty commends itself to Presbyterian and Coptic Christian alike.

Probably the most pervasive criticism of a secular moral-education program in the schools is that it provides no motivation to be moral: not the fear of God or of Hell, and not the love of God and the wish to respect Him by following His law. This argument has implications for moral motivation that are, simply put, false—namely, that the motivation to be the right sort of person must come from fear or from love or respect for some Being. Not only is there nothing inconsistent in supposing that there is no such motivation in a moral person; it is also the case that, at least with respect to fear, *that* motivation is not a moral one. It is prudence, not morality, that leads me to do what is right out of fear that if I do not do it, I will suffer for eternity in Hell. If by encouraging such fears, religious-education programs succeed in imposing certain patterns of behavior on children, it does not follow that the education in question is moral. The person in question will simply do what he is afraid not to do. But that can as well be a prescription for an immoral as for a moral man: such a person is moving outside the realm of morality. He is not honest because of what he recognizes about the demands of honesty, nor is he fair because of what fairness demands, once it is understood what fairness in human relations is. He is honest because if he is not, he will suffer.

Moral motivation may come from love of or respect for a deity, if the deity is the sort of deity that can morally command love and respect. Such love and respect are the next best motivation to that of the person who is the right sort of person because of what he recognizes or realizes is demanded of him as an actor in the world. But since this is what is central and since this realization is not only remotely possible but is often actual, it is hard to understand why it may not be approached directly.

Aside from the constitutional provisions that are designed to protect religious freedom, there are, then, good reasons not to tie moral to religious instruction. An additional reason is this: if it is granted that moral learning need not lean on religious belief, there is good reason to encourage its development in such a way that it not lean too heavily. Religious belief is, in an open society, a society that encourages critical reflection, a notoriously fragile structure. Many reflective persons come to disavow it. But such persons are better off if their realization that they no longer are believers is not the occasion of a moral crisis—a crisis that arises only if their motivation to be moral arises solely from religious sources.

The question of moral motivation and of how it can be strengthened is, of course, a central one for moral education and hence for an approach that emphasizes becoming the right sort of person. There are moral philosophies that, assuming the prevalence of egoistic, selfish desires and attitudes, attempt to bridge from those attitudes and desires to moral attitudes. Thus, in Hobbesian contractarian theories, we move from a state of nature in which egoism is the central motive to a state of society that is held together by essentially the same motive. Kant emphasized the attractive power of the categorical imperative itself; sociological theories emphasize the power of shame and blame in motivating conventionally approved behavior;

some psychological theories find moral motivation in the ascendancy of one or the other part of the psyche; and so on. On the present view, the motivation is there, but it needs to be directed. The assumption from which I begin is that everyone has some character ideals, no matter how ill defined or misguided they may be. People are, in general, concerned about the kind of people they have been, are becoming, and want to be.

This interest in the character of the self can be more or less intense, and it will typically be strongest during just those periods of life in which most can be done about defining one's character: namely, in childhood and youth.

Learning to become the right sort of person is in large part learning not to become the wrong sort: cruel, vindictive, dishonest, unjust, callous, and weak-willed, for example. One must come to be repelled by evidences of these qualities of character, just as one must learn to be attracted by (or anyway appropriately appreciative of) kindness, honesty, courage, and so forth. Why should this not be a part of learning? Why can it not be encouraged by appropriate measures?[5] Appropriate measures would start with moral training, when the child is too young fully to appreciate the reasons why the vices are vices and the virtues are virtues, and would progress to the stage at which the youth can appreciate the rationale that informs the distinctions between vices and virtues. It is, in the end, certain sorts of people that we are repelled and attracted by; and the business of moral education is to make our repulsions and attractions morally defensible ones.

Hume had a great deal to say on the subject of why it is that we are attracted to the qualities of persons that do attract us; and he attributed all such attractions to the usefulness of the qualities in question, either for everyone in general or for the possessor of the quality. I think that this is very close to the mark but that Hume's insight should not be confused with the later utilitarianism of Bentham and Mill. For Hume, a quality can be useful in a number of different ways, not just in the way of increasing or of working toward the increase of the general happiness. Atop Hume's analysis of the reasons why certain qualities are attractive, we need only add some necessary distinctions. Some qualities we recognize as not merely attractive but as essential to common life: minimal honesty, sensitivity, and self-control, for example. Others we appreciate when they are present, because we can see why persons who have them are preferable to persons who do not. The attractiveness or repellency of qualities of character must be seen against the general background of a world in which it is necessary to be judgmental—in which we must choose between people and, correspondingly, must choose between possible selves in the range of possibilities that are open to us as developing beings.

This practical world—the world of choice of persons (and actions and policies)—is what provides the context within which it makes sense to worry about qualities of character. And this context of discussion of qualities of character is what sets off the moral from the psychoanalytic or the generally scientific point of view. The point of moral characterization of a person is not to provide the sort of description of him that will make therapeutic intervention most effective or scientific understanding complete; it is to warn or to reassure us, since we are considering what sort of relations to have with him in a world of action. To care for the child is to prepare him as thoroughly as possible for the practical world, to help him to shape himself appropriately for it, and to appreciate why certain sorts of people are to be preferred to other sorts. Perhaps, in the end, he may be excited by the possibilities that he sees in others and in himself of becoming remarkably or superlatively morally strong, courageous, honest. Moral models, real or imagined, in contemporary life, in films, in novels, in plays, or in history, may become an engaging part of his movement into the world of action.

But it is not merely in caring for the child who is about to enter the practical world that moral education is to be understood. The teacher must care for the practical world as well—the world of rules, roles, practices, policies, and institutions. He is not just teaching the children to cope, to get along, to survive; he is also helping the child to understand that he is not to value those persons and policies and so forth, that erode what is valuable in the common world. The child is being prepared for, by being initiated into, a common and already existent network of rights, obligations, and duties; and he is being led at the same time to value that network or, at any rate, to respect it.

The child must learn that in the practical world—as opposed to the world of therapists and patients, scientists and objects of science, artists and subjects of artistic interest—what is important is what we may (or do or ought to) expect of other people and of ourselves. It is our daily business to assess, to appraise, to judge persons. We want to understand them, but to understand them for purposes of assessment, not out of mere curiosity or evanescent interest. Understanding other persons, as well as ourselves, is, notoriously, one of the most difficult tasks of life. It is a task so important and central in life that it takes on a life of its own: it is the central stuff of drama, film, literature, and history and of several psychological and social sciences and arts. The understanding that concerns the teacher who hopes to help the child to become the right sort of person is an understanding directed, however tacitly, at the judgmental task. The child must grasp the *modes* of judgment and appraisal. While a novelist might devote a trilogy to the investigation of forms of courage, the child must start by being brought very early to recognize that there is such a thing as courage and, at the same time, to value it. He will, inevitably, be taught by example or illustration. He will be encouraged to notice example after example and, at the same time, to admire what is revealed in the examples; and he will be taught to despise cowardice.

It is, I think, obvious enough not to require argument here that two of the most resistant barriers to the child's learning are a narcissistic concern with the self and an obtuseness or callousness about the feelings and interests of others. What may not be so obvious is that there is a third natural tendency to avoid: namely, an undifferentiating, open, and, for a young child, quite natural love of other persons, almost every other person. We sometimes speak as if the ideal morality would be a morality of universal love, but that notion should be welcomed only with reservations.

The teacher who cares for the child and for the common good must surely recognize that it is unfair to both to encourage the development of too unjudgmentally warm a character. Such a character will be grievously disappointed by and will be at the mercy of other less saintly persons. At the same time, love generates love, and openness encourages openness; the delicate balance must be reached differently for different developing persons between being open and loving, on the one hand, and guarded and judgmental, on the other. The general point to be made is that it is unfair to the child to neglect the judgmental side of his character. It is unfair to society not to encourage in the child those capacities of judgment of others that are necessary if the social order is to work for the common good. If the child, when he comes to maturity, is unable to assess people morally, he is by the same token unable to make intelligent decisions about who shall occupy what roles, about what agreements he should or should not enter into—in short, about how to carry on his own life and his share of the public life intelligently, effectively, and with a sense of what a free community requires. He will be a personal and a social disaster.

It is for reasons of this sort that Kant rightly substitutes for the notion of love that of respect and that he (somewhat misleadingly) ties respect for the person to respect for the 'moral law' as it is evident in the person.[6] It is better to enter the world full of respect for others (and the world is better) than it is to enter the world full of undiscriminating love. There is a moral presumption, it may well be argued, that we should have respect for every human being. That is, we should not treat any human being as an object, as a mere means to any end, but should recognize that that being, like ourselves, has feelings, desires, and plans of his own. Nevertheless, it is a rebuttable presumption. Our respect for the other person must be shaded by the extent to which the other has cultivated virtues rather than vices. We cannot be as respectful of the sloth, the coward, and the dishonorable as we are of the energetic, the courageous, and the honorable. This is consistent with saying that as a matter of public morality, legislation and judicial adjudication should always honor the right of every individual not to have his feelings, desires, and plans arbitrarily overridden or interfered with: the circle of individual freedom should have as long a radius as possible.

I t is common in moral philosophy and moral psychology to worry about how the cognitive and affective parts of moral education can be brought together. The notion is that there is the task of deciding what is right or wrong, good or bad; and there is the task of getting up enough steam to go ahead and do what is right or to resist doing what is wrong. On the one hand, we use terms like 'know', 'discover', and 'intuit', and on the other hand, we use terms like 'resolve', 'will', and 'determine'. The gap between the two tasks is only partially a real one. It is true that we sometimes have trouble doing what we ought to do. But the notion should be resisted that there is, in principle, necessarily any such gap. That there is not can be appreciated by noticing that there is another way of talking about the way to enter into moral appraisals—namely, the language of the virtues and the vices.

Here it will be useful to speak of ethological considerations—considerations that concern, at once, the character of the agent (ethos) and the qualities of acts or policies: just, honest, mean, kind, or loyal, for example. It will also be useful to distinguish between appreciating or understanding or realizing something and, on the other hand, merely knowing it. There is a certain distance between knowing that it is wrong to torture people and appreciating its wrongness or realizing it. We can say of a person who knows it that he may not be 'moved by' his knowledge; but a person cannot so naturally be said at once to appreciate or realize the wrongness of torture and to go happily about a career of torture. It is even more useful to put the language of appreciation or realization together with the ethological considerations. Thus, instead of arriving at the knowledge that torture is wrong, the aim of education can be to arrive at the realization that whatever is cruel is so far wrong and that torture is paradigmatically cruel.

If we can assume that the child would like to be the right sort of person and if he can be brought to realize that and to realize why dishonest persons are not the right sort, then it will be enough for him to understand that an act would be a dishonest one and that he does not want to do it. He should not do what would make of him the sort of person that he does not want to be. But the rationale of his refusal to do the dishonest thing is not a narcissistic one. He is not trying merely to improve his image. He is developing a conception of himself that will not allow him to do what is dishonest—or at any rate will make him take the dishonesty of the act into account in making his judgment. The point is that the cognitive-affective gap need not exist for him at all: that there is no bridge to be built, no a priori chasm. By thinking of torture as cruel, he is thinking of it as the sort of thing that he does not want to do, because he does want to be the right sort of person. To see it as cruel *is* to see it as what he does not want to do.

What is built, then, into a moral-education program that emphasizes becoming the right sort of person is the two-directional nature of moral judgment. In agonizing over a choice about what to do or approve, the agent is agonizing at the same time over what he is to be or become. He defines himself in his choices; he does not merely adhere or fail to adhere to some external shadow-legal set of 'moral rules'. Ethological considerations tend to make this two-directional feature of moral judgment plain; nonethological appeals to rules, rights, and the like, can obscure it. It can seem as if what is at issue is like a case before a court, where issues of precedence and constitutionality are all that count. But what is always at issue in every hard choice is what self-assessment would be warranted by this option or by that one.

What I have called helping the child to become the right sort of person will be criticized as a reversion to the 'bag of virtues' approach to moral education.[7] That approach is typified, I suppose, by the drumming in of the Boy Scout pledge to be honest, trustworthy, and on and on; by the morally uplifting stories in the McGuffey reader; and by the kind of moral instruction that was current in American schools and colleges during the nineteenth century—an education that too easily inculcated a kind of 'spiritual egotism' in which the child was encouraged to think all too much about the ideal shaping of a beautiful character and too little about the rights and duties that he had in a moral community.

The strength of this sort of criticism rests on two points: that the sort of education I advocate is not undergirded by some systematic moral theory and that it encourages the positively immoral narcissism of the 'spiritual egotist'. However, I do not think that either point is well taken.

In the first place, as I have suggested in chapters 3 and 4, the paradigms of systematic contemporary theories—utilitarianism, formalism, and contract theory—are themselves full of difficulty if they pose as having justificatory powers in moral decision making. Since they define moral problems differently and in inconsistent ways, there is the question of whether they can speak to the same moral problems at all. And since they themselves rest on truisms that have no greater claim to moral considerations than the ethological considerations, it is at least worth asking why we should not move directly to the considerations. On the other hand, it is not the case that the ethological approach to moral education and justification makes use of an arbitrarily assembled 'bag' of virtues (and a black bag of vices). For a trait to count as a virtue, there must be reason to think that the person who bears that trait is quite generally preferable to the person who does not. In thinking what the most general grounds of preference are, we assemble a coherent set of assumptions about 'the human situation', both individual and communal. We sharpen our awareness, that is, of the need for certain qualities of character if we are not to pay impossibly high prices in misery and anarchy and if we are to have any chance at all of advancing toward states of affairs that all of us want, whatever else we want.

Secondly, as I have pointed out above, the interest that the child develops in not being dishonest, say, is an interest that rests, if his moral learning has managed to stay on the right track, on his realizing why dishonesty is wrong, on his appreciating that to be dishonest is to be the wrong sort of person. It is not therefore a form of moral preening for him to be interested in the question of whether by acting in a certain way he would be dishonest.

An advantage of the present approach to the problem of moral learning is that it does not rest on too high, and therefore on too empty or confusing, an abstraction, such as conformity, obedience, respect, autonomy, self-realization, perfection, or whatever. A common difficulty of all such modes of conceiving the purpose of moral education is that it all depends on what, if any, substance is then placed under the abstract and substanceless abstraction: the 'governing principle' or the 'highest value'. Autonomous agents may legislate a consistently repugnant set of rules for themselves. Conformity is desirable only to the extent that the rules to which conformation is to be achieved are desirable. And so on. But by contrast, injustice, cruelty, vindictiveness, dishonesty, or selfishness are undesirable, period.

Some abstract theories do have this to offer to the teacher: they provide procedural hints or suggestions about how the moral person may think about difficult problems.[8] In this sense, they are as useful as the Golden Rule. In this sense, the utilitarian emphasis on thinking through to the consequences, the formalist focus on the consistency of self-legislated rules, and the contractarian point that prior understandings should be given their due are all aids to the reflections of an already morally sensitized person—one who abhors cruelty, values honesty, and so on. They are aids to the thought of the right sort of person, but they are no substitute for the kind of help that a child needs in order to become that sort of person. They might, given the appropriate underlying dispositions, improve his moral judgment, by offering formulae to collect and order his deliberations. Unhappily, however, because of the exclusive claims that autonomy, self-realization, and so forth, make to having justificatory force, they cannot yield place to one another as so many equally valid points of view that should inform moral judgment.

Questions about the rightness or wrongness of actions or policies typically need to be opened up or cashed into more manageable questions. Unless the action or policy is paradigmatically or self-evidently wrong and unless children may be taught that this just is not to be done ever and thus may be supplied with a 'rule', a more instructive way to approach the matter is to raise the question of how, in what respect, the proposed action or policy would be wrong. This leads beyond the summary conclusions to the ethological considerations on which they must, in the end anyway, rest: that it would be dishonest, selfish, unfair, and so forth. To say that an action would be wrong but that it is not wrong in any of these ethological respects would be to speak unintelligibly. To say that it would be unfair is to imply that it is so far wrong but is to leave open the possibility that there may be other respects in which it would be the most defensible course of action. Sometimes unfairness to one group may be required if we are to be fair to another group or if we are to be honest in our dealings with a third group, and so on. It can hardly be to the child's disadvantage to be introduced early to the possibility that ethological considerations may be hard to bring into balance.

I f we may take it for granted that the child wants to be the right sort of person and to be helped to reason out what the right sort is, then we know generally the kind of help that the child needs. How it is to be supplied him is beyond my capacity to say. The best I can do is to offer suggestions that may or may not prove useful to teachers in the schools.

(1) The teacher must first prepare himself by thinking through what his responsibilities are to the child and to society. His responsibility to the child is to help him acquire dispositions that he needs in the world he is entering. The child needs these dispositions or virtues because, without them, he will rightly either not be preferred or will be avoided by other persons. He will not be worthy of preference or will deserve to be avoided. The child must therefore understand why the dispositions are rightly expected, and he must be helped to acquire them. The teacher's responsibility to society is to act as its agent in initiating the child into the modes of feeling, thought, and action that society has a right to expect of the child.

(2) The teacher must do what he can to make himself an intelligent judge of character. He must train himself to think of character, to appraise character development, to be a 'sympathetic judge' of character. He must be aware of the character that he himself presents to the children whose

characters are going to be influenced by him—by him as a model. He must learn as well as he can to distinguish matters of doctrine from nondoctrinal, ethological, matters. He must not be confused about what may properly be demanded of the right sort of person, and he must be forthright in demanding it. But he must take care not to try to inculcate moral beliefs or doctrines as if they were beyond question, including the central doctrines of democracy.

(3) At the same time, the teacher must be aware that there are certain traits of character that are better suited than others to the democratic tradition: tolerance, respect for persons, respect for doctrines other than his own, respect for the outcome of fair decision procedures. These traits are of course valuable in any other society, as well.

(4) The teacher must recognize that if he does not exercise his judgment on the developing character of his students, they will be sole judges of each other. The qualities that peer judgment approves will not necessarily be in the child's interest or in the interest of society. There will be a tendency for the strongest or the most charming to prevail as models. Children can be made aware that there are alternative models of what qualities are to be appreciated, even if they are less immediately appealing than sheer strength, bravado, and charm.

(5) The teacher must avoid a rule-worshiping attitude: he must distinguish what is important in the human situation from what is peripheral. The fewer rules, the better, if intelligent dispositions can be made to take their place. Considerate children, for example, do not need a rule that they must clean up for the next art class. The purpose of rules should be as much to develop the right dispositions as to make the common life smoother. The right dispositions are not developed by multiplying the number of rules.

(6) The teacher must beware of overt techniques or tricks in moral education. The aim must be to make of himself the right sort and to improve his judgment of who is and is not the right sort. Then the children will benefit.

(7) The teacher must be an enthusiastic appreciator of evidences of the right sort of dispositions, but he must be extremely cautious about depreciation, either explicit or tacit. Firmness in requiring adherence to standards need not

involve any depreciation. What are rightly depreciated are attitudes and modes of action, not persons.

(8) The teacher must learn what he can about what he may and may not expect of children; he must not be the sort of perfectionist who induces pathological guilt feelings.

(9) The teacher must try to forget the nonsense that he may have learned about not being 'judgmental'; he must instead do what he can to develop a sense for when moral judgment is and is not appropriate and for what the ethological parameters of moral judgment are. And he must recognize that as a person in a very special position of trust, he must do what he is able to do to encourage in children the understanding that some dispositions are vices and that others are virtues.

This brings us back around to the door through which we entered in the first chapter. While there are moral quandaries and dilemmas in life, they arise with the appropriate intensity only for the right sort of person. If, in the order of exposition, we have come to moral education last, nevertheless it has a strong claim to be first in the ethical order of importance. Once we recognize that ethics is not best reduced to the search for a universal solvent of moral dilemmas, we are free to explore the varied and rich texture of moral talk and thought. We are in a better position to appreciate the intentions of those philosophers who, in the long tradition of ethics, were concerned to distinguish between the kinds of persons who are worthy of preference and those who are not. And with whatever insights we can attain on that subject, we may begin to think how we can be better persons—and how we can encourage the young to be better than we are.

Notes

CHAPTER 1. INTRODUCTION

1. By 'he', 'him', 'his', please understand 'he or she', 'him or her', and 'his or hers'. To my ear, the use of the masculine is less distracting. I hope that it will not be found offensive.

CHAPTER 2. QUANDARY ETHICS

1. The distinction is very similar to Kant's distinction between perfect and imperfect duties. I have avoided making it in Kant's terms because of the possibilities for confusion inherent in Kant's association of the former with one form of ethics, 'the doctrine of right', and the latter with another form.

CHAPTER 3. THE RELEVANCE
OF THE STANDARD THEORIES

1. My remarks should be general enough to apply to any form of utilitarianism or contractarian theory and to formalistic ''Kantian'' theories that understand problems about what to do as problems concerning one's duty under a set of self-legislated universal rules. They apply to these theories when they are consistently held as mutually exclusive alternatives. They usually are held to be mutually exclusive, but they are not often held consistently. For the consistent utilitarian, consideration of (the preferred type of) consequence must *govern* when decisions are to be made. The governing considerations for consistent contractarian theorists concern the obligation to abide by agreements freely entered into. Consistent formalists allow only appropriately qualified rules to govern. To say of a particular kind of considera-

tion that it governs is to say, at least, that no consideration is relevant in the justification of a moral conclusion unless it is, or is derivable from, the kind of consideration in question.

I hold that the standard theories, consistently held, are therefore reductive in that they rule out, as relevant, considerations that are intuitively relevant. It is this characteristic that results in their determining what is to count as a moral problem. Those and only those problems count as moral that can potentially be resolved by appeal solely to the favored kind of consideration.

2. John Rawls, "Two Concepts of Rules," *Philosophical Review* 64 (1955).

3. G. E. Moore, *Principia Ethica* (Cambridge University Press, 1903), chap. 1.

4. W. D. Ross, *The Right and the Good* (Oxford University Press, 1930), chap. 2.

5. It would be possible for a Stoic to become a theorist in the following way: he could count as a moral problem only what has to do with the maintenance of his own serenity of mind. Then he is an egoistic consequentialist of a certain sort. But I assume that this would amount to a misrepresentation of the Stoic pattern. It is a pattern, and it includes a whole network of interrelated ideals and standards of nobility, high-mindedness, self-control, and so on. It is not a means/end nightmare in which nothing whatever counts but serenity. Serenity that could be achieved at the cost of ignoble deeds would not be acceptable; and serenity is consistent with recognizing the humanity and the claims, under natural law, of other persons.

6. Cf., e.g., Mary Hesse, *Models and Analogy in Science* (University of Notre Dame Press, 1966); or Peter Achinstein, "Models, Analogies and Theories," *Philosophy of Science* 31 (Oct. 1964): 328–49.

CHAPTER 4. THE JUSTIFICATORY POWERS OF THE STANDARD THEORIES

1. W. D. Ross, *The Right and the Good* (Oxford University Press, 1930), cf., esp., chap. 2, "What Makes Right Acts Right?"

2. Nietzsche argues, in a famous passage, that "almost everything we call 'higher culture' is based on the spiritualization of *cruelty* on its becoming more profound: this is my proposition. That 'savage animal' has not really been 'mortified'; it lives and flourishes, it has merely become—divine" (*Beyond Good and Evil* [Random House, 1966], trans. Walter Kaufman, sect. 229). The

savage tendencies of days of yore, Nietzsche argues, crop up again in metaphysics, in tragedy, in bullfights, and in bloody revolutions. In all of these we find secret thrills and gratifications at the cruelty that is either hinted at or shown forth. But this is not convincing. Indeed, one of the dangers of cruelty is that we may find relish in it, secretly desire it, or even glorify it. It does not follow that cruelty is morally acceptable. Nietzsche's response would be that it is unacceptable only in a slave morality, a morality that is itself unacceptable. But that is, I think, to beg the question at issue. For how are we to distinguish an acceptable from an unacceptable morality except by an appeal to moral truisms? We do not show that cruelty is unacceptable because it is enshrined in an acceptable morality; we judge moralities by what they accept as truistic. A morality that does not recognize the wrongness of cruelty is, so far, morally unacceptable.

3. It is possible to argue with a Nietzsche in this way, if we can avoid the question-begging appeals to supposedly superior moralities. Despite his sweeping rhetoric about the transvaluation of values, Nietzsche does value honesty (*Beyond Good and Evil*, sect. 227). This is the quality that enables us to see and live by (or may some day enable 'men of free spirit' to see and live by) a code that is superior to the humane and Christian 'slave morality'. The question, then, is what is there to be revealed to the honest inquirer as to whether cruelty, even though it attracts, is good.

4. Cf. H. L. A. Hart, *The Concept of Law* (Oxford University Press, 1961), pp. 55–56.

5. Cf. R. M. Hare, *Freedom and Reason* (Oxford University Press, 1963), sec. 9.8.

6. John Stuart Mill, *A System of Logic*, many editions, first published in 1843.

CHAPTER 5. TWO CHEERS FOR MENO:
THE DEFINITION OF THE VIRTUES

1. Cf. Herbert Morris's suggestive remarks on fairness in "Persons and Punishment," *Monist* 52, no. 4 (1968).

2. G. H. von Wright, *The Varieties of Goodness* (Humanities Press, 1963), pp. 147ff.

3. Lester H. Hunt, "Character and Thought," *American Philosophical Quarterly* 15, no. 3 (1978).

4. Maurice Mandelbaum, *The Phenomenology of Moral Experience* (Johns Hopkins Press, 1969), p. 150.

5. Ibid., p. 141.

6. Ibid., p. 144.
7. Alasdair MacIntyre, *After Virtue: A Study in Moral Theory* (University of Notre Dame Press, 1981).
8. James D. Wallace, *Virtues and Vices* (Cornell University Press, 1978), cf., esp., chaps. 1 and 4.
9. Peter Geach, *The Virtues* (Cambridge University Press, 1977); and Philippa Foot, "Virtues and Vices," in *Virtues and Vices and Other Essays in Moral Philosophy* (University of California Press, 1978), pp. 1–18.
10. Lawrence Kohlberg, "Education for Justice: A Modern Statement of the Platonic View," in *Moral Education: Five Lectures* (Harvard University Press, 1970).

CHAPTER 6. A DEFENSE OF PERFECTIONISM

1. I have in mind particularly the theories that have some claim to be, in contemporary discussion, the standard ones: utilitarianism, contract theory, and 'formal' theories. By 'formal' theory I mean the sort of theory I mention below as following from an acceptance of some version of the first formulation of the categorical imperative: a theory that holds that there is some very tight relation between an act's being morally acceptable and its being in accordance with a rule that can be universalized for everyone. There is, of course, a minority of 'naturalists' who have insisted on the moral relevance of the virtue and vice considerations.
2. The perfection can also be of a state of affairs or condition of the world or some part of it, including sentient and nonsentient beings. I will consider only the perfectionism that has persons and their activities and undertakings as its object.
3. There are consequential versions of perfectionism according to which an act is morally acceptable if it is conducive to, or at least is not detrimental to, the attainment of some ideal state of affairs. However, the ideal state of affairs is usually conceived of as one in which a given set of perfectionistic standards are adhered to— justice, kindness, etc. I will, for present purposes, focus only on directly standard-abiding perfectionism.
4. Geoffrey Warnock, *The Object of Morality* (Methuen & Co., 1971), p. 86.
5. In fact, to be the sort of person that utilitarian theory approves of, he need not be a utilitarian at all. Whatever his motives or theory preference, he is approved only as an effective contributor to the general happiness. This point is recognized by the classical utilitarians and is emphasized by their contemporary critics.

6. I am not sure that anyone has ever held such a theory, but the persistence of the criticism indicates that opponents of 'perfectionism' suppose that someone has. D. H. Meyer, in *The Instructed Conscience: The Shaping of the American National Ethic* (University of Pennsylvania Press, 1972), cites (p. 82) the teachings of James Harris Fairchild, who holds that there is no distinction to be made between obligation and supererogation, that "there can be no meritorious works that are not obligatory." This is the culmination of one tradition of nineteenth-century moral instruction (the Oberlin perfectionistic one). It follows, from this position, that we are morally obligated to attain perfection, if by perfection we mean doing every meritorious thing that we are capable of doing.

7. John Rawls, *A Theory of Justice* (Harvard University Press), pp. 327–29.

8. Cf., e.g., Victor Gourevitch, "Rawls on Justice," *Review of Metaphysics* 28 (Mar. 1975): 485–519; Kai Nielsen, "The Choice between Perfectionism and Rawlsian Contractarianism," *Interpretation* 6 (May 1977): 132–39; and Vinit Haksar, *Equality, Liberty, and Perfectionism* (Oxford University Press, 1979), chap. 10.

9. Cf. Joel Feinberg, "Absurd Self-fulfillment," in *Time and Cause*, ed. Peter van Inwagen (D. Reidel, 1980), pp. 255–81; also Daniel Yankelovich, *New Rules* (Random House, 1981), pt. 2, "Experiments in Self-fulfillment."

10. It is a feature of the Thesis that the outcome of reasoning from virtue considerations can be indeterminate. A course of action can have high grades for loyalty but low ones for justice. To say that the virtue considerations govern moral acceptability is not to say that they determine, in every case, what we may do, morally speaking.

11. John Dewey, *Human Nature and Conduct* (George Allen & Unwin, 1922), p. 7.

12. Cf. Meyer, *Instructed Conscience*, pp. 83–84.

13. Ibid., p. 115.

14. Hare holds that there is a gap: that of any "secondarily evaluative condemnatory adjective," F (such as 'dishonest', presumably—Hare chooses the term 'lazy'), we can always ask about a proposed action, "Granted that it would be F, would it be *wrong*?" (*Moral Thinking* [Oxford University Press, 1981], p. 18). But it is not clear what the sense would be of asking "Granted that the act would not accord with the standards set by the virtue considerations, would it be wrong?" The question becomes progressively less meaningful as virtue considerations are added, thus closing out senses in which someone could say, "I know that it is dishonest, unkind, and . . . nevertheless it is right."

CHAPTER 7. IDEALS OF VIRTUE AND
MORAL OBLIGATION: GANDHI

1. Robert Payne, *The Life and Death of Mahatma Gandhi* (E. P. Dutton & Co., 1969), p. 24; hereafter cited as *LDM*.

2. In what follows, I use the terms 'obligation' and 'duty' more or less interchangeably, since a distinction between them is not crucial. Ordinarily, I would think of duties as arising out of the requirements of the roles one plays, such as father or teacher, and of obligations as arising out of commitments one has made, such as contracts, agreements, promises.

3. Ayn Rand, *The Virtue of Selfishness* (Signet Books, 1961), p. vii. She does not specify which dictionary she reads, but in mine, *Webster's Third New International*, 'selfishness' turns out to be "concern for one's own welfare or advantage at the expense of or in disregard of others."

4. *Webster's Third New International Dictionary.*

CHAPTER 8. ON AVOIDING MORAL INDOCTRINATION

1. John Wilson's "Education and Indoctrination" and R. M. Hare's "Adolescents into Adults" will be found in *Aims in Education*, ed. T. H. B. Hollins (Manchester University Press, 1964), pp. 24–46 and 47–70.

2. The situation is, for Wilson, somewhere beyond dire. "We know how to do science," he tells us, "but we do not know how to do metaphysics or morals—this is sufficiently obvious to an intelligent child, though he might not be able to state it clearly" (p. 30).

3. R. M. Hare, *Language of Morals* (*LM*) (Oxford University Press, 1952), chap. 4, and *Freedom and Reason* (*FR*) (Oxford University Press, 1963), chaps. 3 and 6.

4. *FR*, chap. 6.

5. *LM*, chap. 4.

6. Ibid., chap. 1, secs. 3.6, 4.1, and 4.3.

7. Aristotle, *Ethica Nicomachea*, 1112a.

CHAPTER 9. ON BECOMING THE RIGHT SORT

1. The tendency toward one-virtue ethics as the basis for a theory of moral education is a venerable one. The summary claims of justice are advanced by Plato in *The Republic*. Kant's moral philosophy could be read (cf., esp., the first section of the

Foundations of the Metaphysics of Morals) as a paean to conscientiousness. *The* utilitarian virtue is benevolence.

2. For an able defense of the social need to inculcate certain dispositions as virtues cf. Andrew Oldenquist, " 'Indoctrination' and 'Societal Suicide,' " *Public Interest,* no. 63 (Spring 1981): 81–94.

3. The Kohlbergian assessments of moral development have, I think rightly, been criticized as overly 'cognitive' in their approach. Cf., esp., Jon Moline, "Classical Ideas about Moral Education," *Character* 2, no. 8 (June 1981): 1–8.

4. A considerable literature is developing on the subject of the sort of moral education that is permissible or desirable in a democratic state. Cf., e.g., Michael Schleifer, "Moral Education and Indoctrination," *Ethics* 86, no. 2 (Jan. 1976): 154–63; Patricia M. Lines, *Religious and Moral Values in Public Schools: A Constitutional Analysis* (Education Commission of the States, Denver, Colo., Jan. 1981); Brian Crittenden, *Form and Content in Moral Education* (Ontario Institute for Studies in Education, Toronto, 1972); and William J. Bennett and Edwin J. Delattre, "Moral Education in the Schools," *Public Interest,* no. 50 (Winter 1978): 81–98.

5. Cf. the second section of the *Foundations.*

6. Cf. Lawrence Kohlberg, "Education for Justice," in *Moral Education: Five Lectures* (Harvard University Press, 1970), p. 59.

7. E.g., R. M. Hare's *Freedom and Reason* (Oxford University Press, 1963).

8. A theory of moral reasoning, and thus by implication a theory of the development of moral judgment, that has been particularly influential on the development of the present approach is W. D. Ross's *The Right and the Good* (Oxford University Press, 1930). Ross emphasizes the mutually irreducible 'prima facie duties' that must be balanced in deciding what to do. My own emphasis is on 'ethological considerations'. Both approaches are 'lateral' or 'network' theories that do not claim to have found some single 'foundation' for moral judgment.

Index